"*How To Buy A Franchise* is an outstanding guide for the prospective franchise buyer. This book comprehensively reviews the steps a franchise buyer should take and the information that he or she should acquire and understand before a purchase decision is made. *How To Buy A Franchise* lists the government agencies, organizations and other resource providers that are good sources of information. Finally, this book contains excellent advice and guidance for a franchisee in his or her relationship with a franchisor. I highly recommend this book to prospective franchise buyers and existing franchisees."
—Lewis G. Rudnick, *partner, Rudnick & Wolfe; general counsel to the International Franchise Association; editor of the Journal of International Franchising and Distribution Law*

"The most readable, practical and complete book that I have seen on the subject of purchasing a franchise. I strongly recommend it as must reading for anyone interested in buying a franchise for the first time."
—Stephen R. Buchenroth, *attorney and former Chairman of the Franchise Committee of the Small Business Section of the American Bar Association*

"In his book, Jim Meaney offers a first-rate guide to evaluating and selecting a franchise. He puts the emphasis on getting it right, rather than on simply getting it done, and encourages investors to be thorough and critical in their evaluation of a franchised business. There are no guarantees in any business, including franchising, but Meaney's book gives investors an essential framework for evaluating the potential of a franchise. A great read for any would-be franchise investor."
—Matthew R. Shay, *Vice President and Chief Counsel, International Franchise Association*

"If you're thinking of buying a franchise, take the time to read this book. Meaney gives you a thorough, but practical and easy to read, roadmap of how you should go about analyzing your choices and making your decision."
—John R. F. Baer, attorney, Sonnenschein, Nath & Rosenthal

"Jim Meaney's book is an excellent road map for anyone considering the purchase of a franchise. I highly recommend it!"
—Herb Hedden, *Contributing editor, Advising Small Businesses, Franchising Chapters, West Group, franchise attorney*

"Invaluable advice for anyone contemplating the purchase of a franchise. Read this book before signing any documents committing you to a franchise."
—Colin Gabriel, *author of How to Sell Your Business—And Get What You Want!*

"This is yet another fine book on getting a good franchise, but it goes further than simply reflecting the "spin" provided by most sellers of franchises. Mr. Meaney has used several tools, namely, words that will be fully understood by almost every qualified applicant. It explores the major pitfalls that usually abound in the complicated franchise agreement and the pre-sale disclosure prospectus (the UFOC) and differences between the UFOC and the actual franchise contract. It stresses the promises and actual performance since that is the unknown in which the franchisee places his faith and trust in the franchisor, exactly as planned and frequently repeated by the franchisor and its highly trained salesperson. There is just enough "legal" jargon to alert the wary and hopefully to lead legal advisors to serious study and application of statutes, common law and local practice that will help in each case.

Many authorities have noted that it is almost impossible to divert a buyer who has decided to buy into a particular franchise. This volume makes a valiant effort to teach that great caution is essential. The missing link occurs when the prospect fails to carefully read and heed Mr. Meaney's advice."
—Harold Brown, *attorney and author of numerous books and articles on franchising and franchise law, e.g., monthly New York Law Journal articles, and "Franchising: Realities and Remedies," (Law Journ. Seminars-Press Rev. Ed. 1998)*

The *New Entrepreneur* Series

HOW TO BUY A FRANCHISE

AN EXPERIENCED FRANCHISE LAWYER SHOWS HOW TO FIND, EVALUATE AND NEGOTIATE FOR THE *RIGHT* FRANCHISE

JAMES A. MEANEY

pilot books . . . guides to the good life, all your life

9-2-99

Copyright © 1999 by
PILOT BOOKS
127 Sterling Avenue
Greenport, New York 11944

Library of Congress Catalog Card Number: 98-30264

Names of franchises and/or products mentioned in this book known to
be or suspected of being trademarks or service marks are capitalized.
The use of a trademark or service mark in this book should not be
regarded as affecting the validity of any trademark or service mark.

Library of Congress Cataloging in Publication Data
Meaney, James A., 1952 -
    How to Buy a Franchise: an experienced franchise lawyer shows
how to find, evaluate and negotiate for the right franchise / by James
A. Meaney.
        p. cm.
    Includes bibliographical references and index.
    ISBN: 0-87576-217-4 (alk. paper)
    1. Franchises (retail trade) I. Title
    HF5429.23.M43 1999
    658.8'708 dc21   98-30264
                                                                              CIP

ABOUT THE AUTHOR

James A. Meaney, an attorney with Alkon, Rhea & Hart, St. Croix, United States Virgin Islands, has been named in The Best Lawyers in America (Franchising) since 1994. His practice includes representation of franchisees and franchisors, franchise litigation, preparation of franchise disclosure documents, general business law and litigation, and personal injury litigation.

Mr. Meaney is a member of the American Bar Association's Forum Committee on Franchising and served as the first Chairperson of the Columbus (Ohio) Bar Association's Franchise and Distribution Law Committee from 1992 to 1994. He served on the Columbus Bar Association's Board of Governors from 1995 to 1997. In April, 1997, he relocated his practice to Christiansted, St. Croix in the U.S. Virgin Islands.

Mr. Meaney is the author of "Evaluating and Buying a Franchise" (Pilot Books, 1987). In addition to frequent lectures on franchising-related topics, Mr. Meaney has been a contributing editor of Advising Small Businesses (Franchising Chapters), Clark, Boardman, Callaghan (1992 to 1997). His other writings on franchising include:

"Getting Your Message Across: Learning to Speak So That Your Franchisor (or Franchisees) Will Listen", American Bar Association Forum on Franchising, 1996 Mid-Year Meeting

"Choice of Law: A New Paradigm For Franchise Relationships", 15 Franchise Law Journal, 75 (Winter 1996).

"Representing Franchisees", American Bar Association Forum on Franchising, 1997 Annual Forum (Co-Author-October 1996).

Mr. Meaney is a cum laude graduate of the University of Dayton School of Law. He was Section Chief of the Ohio Consumer Frauds and Crimes Division, Ohio Attorney General's Office from 1982 through 1984, where he first became involved in franchise regulation and litigation.

CONTENTS

Introduction   1

SECTION I
FRANCHISING AND YOU   5

1   Why Buy a Franchise?   7
2   What Is A Franchise?   17
3   How to Find the Right Franchise for *You*   23

SECTION II
EVALUATING YOUR CHOICES   35

4   Protection Under the FTC Regulation
    and State Laws   37
5   The Disclosure Statement   49
6   Financial Feasibility   67
7   Professional Assistance   73
8   Franchise Salespeople and Brokers   79
9   The History Of The Franchisor   83
10   Investigating Existing Franchisees   91
11   Earnings Claims   97

SECTION III
NEGOTIATING FOR AND BUYING
A FRANCHISE   103

12   Understanding and Negotiating
    The Franchise Agreement   105

13 Your Relationship With The Franchisor   133
14 Franchisee Input and Franchisee Associations   137

Conclusion   143

APPENDIX A
Sample Uniform Franchise Offering Circular   145

APPENDIX B
Sample Franchise Agreement   185

Index   217

INTRODUCTION

If you are reading this book, you are probably thinking about buying a franchise. So are many other people today, and for good reason. Franchising has taken the world by storm. New franchises come into existence every day and—from Topeka to Timbuktu—the names of well-known franchise companies have become household words.

Many people consider franchising the epitome of the American dream, an opportunity for financial success unparalleled in U.S. business history. A report issued by the U.S. House of Representative's Committee on Small Business *(Franchising in the U.S. Economy: Prospects and Promises)* reflects these sentiments: "Franchising has been called the most dynamic business arrangement since the emergence of the corporation a century ago. It is heralded as a 'dominating force' in the distribution of goods and services and the 'wave of the future' for the U.S. marketplace." By the year 2000, according to *Time Magazine,* franchising will be the "primary method of doing business" in America.

But a word of caution. During the years since franchising became the rage, there have been many times when honest, hard-working people have simply been duped by scam artists. One sad example comes to mind:

A middle-aged couple was interested in starting a business on the side while they kept their regular jobs. They were intrigued by an ad in their local newspaper reading: Earn Big Money While Keeping Your Regular Job—Invest In Your Own Vending Machine

Franchise Business. The ad went on to promise that, by establishing a vending machine business, you would be on the road to independent wealth in no time.

When they followed-up, the seller of the opportunity assured them that by making a $20,000.00 investment in the machines and start-up inventory, they could build the business step-by-step into a successful empire. In addition, by joining the "We've Got Your Franchise System", they would share in the proven format and techniques that were the keys to success. He showed them pictures of his luxurious warehouses in a neighboring state filled with rows of spanking new machines just waiting for a home. He presented them with lists of potential locations in their area where his demographic studies showed people would just kill for vending products. And finally, he used the BIG HOOK: "Oh, and by the way folks, this is a no lose proposition, if you don't succeed, I'll return your investment, no questions asked". They were sold.

The eager buyers wrote the check and sat back to wait, excited by the prospect of beginning their new venture. In a few weeks, as promised, the seller delivered the vending machines—but there was a small problem. The machines appeared to be second-hand, nowhere near as glamorous as the bright, shiny ones shown in the sales pictures. When the buyers called the seller to complain, he quickly apologized, told them he'd meant to call them ahead of time—yes, there was a temporary shortage of new machines but they could get started with these and as soon as the new ones arrived he would replace them. He also told them that he had included their "Initial Route Slip" in with the paperwork for the machines and they should begin securing their locations immediately.

Temporarily satisfied with this explanation, and still "pumped" at the thought of having their own business, the buyers rose at the crack of dawn to establish their locations. To their dismay, the first turned out to be an old, closed gas station. At the next, a small country grocery store, they were told by the owner that he charged $20.00 a month rent and that they had to purchase all the products to stock the machines from his store. And on they went throughout the course of the day, decidedly discouraged by their lack of success. They did manage to place 2 machines at the small grocery store and were able to get the owner to go for a 2-for-1 rent deal.

As they pulled into the driveway that evening, the phone was ringing. It was the seller who wasted no time reassuring them. He was certain they'd had a tough day, he said sympathetically—"the first days are always the toughest." Buoyed by his interest and astute knowledge, the buyers were able to place their other 8 machines during the course of the next two weeks. Over the next month their machines generated revenues of $100.00. After paying the rent to the grocer and figuring their inventory costs, they calculated their profit for the month—$13.13.

Knowing this was a bad omen, they decided to get their money back and look for something else. When they rang up the seller, an electronic operator informed them that "this is no longer a working number." When they complained to state officials whose jobs, supposedly, were to help bilked investors, they learned that they were not alone—25 others had fallen for the same routine and were out $20,000.00 in exchange for a few worthless vending machines.

The message is clear. Even though franchising has gained a reputation as *the* preferred method of doing business in America—if not the world—all franchise opportunities are not created equal, and success is not around every franchise corner. The same Committee report referred to earlier, noted that many of the abuses and failures seen in franchising come from an "informational imbalance" that exists between franchisors and franchise buyers.

Don't fall prey to scam artists. Exercise caution in your business affairs—especially if it is the first time. Learn how to investigate a business opportunity so that you go into it with your eyes wide open. Guard against emotional decisions by relying on the well-proven ways of Sherlock Holmes—investigate, investigate and investigate. The process starts here.

We will begin with some basic franchise history and principles, and the distinctions between a franchise, business opportunity, dealership and distributorship. Next, we will explore how to determine the franchise opportunity that best suits *you*. Then, since it is imperative that buyers know how to research the franchise company as well as the opportunity itself, we will show you what facts to obtain and how to:

- analyze financial and sales information
- investigate earnings claims made by the franchisor

We will discuss how to negotiate the franchise agreement and, finally, the factors involved in the ongoing relationship with the franchisor.

To form a successful, ongoing relationship with your new franchising partner, one that has the potential to give you the profit and fulfillment you want, you must be extremely careful that you are making the right decision and handling the transaction properly. This book will put you on the right path.

To maximize the value of this book and your franchise learning experience, we have included a working appendix at the end. The appendix contains a sample Disclosure Document (from which some non-pertinent information has been deleted) and Franchise Agreement. As you will learn, these documents are the heart of any franchise purchase. During our discussion we will refer to the appendix—follow along to enhance your franchise education.

1

FRANCHISING AND *YOU*

WHY BUY
A FRANCHISE?

Most people buy a franchise because they feel it is less risky than starting a business from scratch. They recognize that their work experience has not prepared them with the knowledge or skills needed to begin and run a business of their own. In addition, many are unwilling to spend time, effort and money reinventing what is already available.

Franchising is also attractive because, to some extent, a franchise is a cooperative, a community of common interests—from centralized national advertising to common products, operating procedures and quality control standards. Because of the protective nature of franchising—with its intensive training programs, written standards and procedures and national name recognition —people, who otherwise would not have risked entering the business world, have taken the leap and opened their own businesses, and done well.

Government statistics bear this out. Although it has been the subject of recent debate, the chance of surviving in a small business is greatly enhanced by membership in a franchising system. The failure rate is reported to be far lower than that of small businesses unsupported by a franchising parent.

Today, more than one-third of all retail businesses are part of a franchise system. By some estimates, this figure will increase to one-half of retail businesses by the turn of the century. Based upon previous industry predictions, combined annual franchise sales will be well over $1 trillion dollars at the dawning of the 21st century.

Originally, it was *repackaging* existing products and services that resulted in some of the most successful franchise systems around today (think of how many hamburger places existed before McDonald's helped make fast food a way of life). Tomorrow's success stories will probably come from capitalizing on new ideas and new technologies.

There seems to be no limit to where and how the franchising concept is applied these days. Real estate, clothing, sports equipment, computer goods and services, packaging services, business services and lodging—these are only some of the hundreds of businesses that use franchising to distribute their goods and services.

International franchising is the next wave. As franchise systems saturate the United States, they look for new opportunities in new markets. Using modern communication and computer technology, franchisors are able to cast a wider net; there are no boundaries. The *info*structure of the 1990's is likely to catapult franchising into the next century with as much vigor as the *infra*structure of the 1950's did in the later half of the 20th Century.

The following are descriptions of the elements usually responsible for a franchising system's success, and some of the reasons why buying a franchise can be a sound investment:

DEFINED/PROVEN BUSINESS FORMAT

What most franchisors are selling is a *defined and proven business format* or method of operation. Although some offer a unique product or service, many franchisors have simply come up with a "new way to slice bread". The founder of Dunkin' Donuts was recently quoted as saying: "Howard Johnson's didn't invent the ice cream cone. Colonel Sanders didn't invent fried chicken. I didn't invent coffee and doughnuts. We just did it better, we had a passion for building a concept".

It has been said that "the simpler the idea the better the franchise". What each of the business leaders mentioned by Dunkin' Donuts' founder did was *develop a proven, recognizable format that was easily duplicated.* They standardized the presentation of their products and the services that went along with them. This is the essence of a proven format in the world of franchising and at the top of the list of reasons for franchising's success. Many of the original franchises began with people who operated their own independent business, refined it, and demonstrated—to themselves and others—that it could be successful.

A *defined format* is what is passed on to franchisees and strictly enforced. It is what creates a positive public image and identification. It is the prime building block of a successful franchise.

Today, while many systems still have grass root beginnings, franchise-making has become big business. Major corporations buy and sell franchise systems like so many pieces on a huge chess board. But, at the heart of every successful franchise system, you will still find a proven format.

SPECIALIZATION

Another reason franchising has found such a solid niche in our modern economy is that it caters to *specialized needs.* Many American consumers no longer want a muffler installed by a service station, a hamburger from a diner, a pizza from someone who won't deliver it within 30 minutes, or their hair cut by a local barber. Specialists, it seems, "do it better" and the franchise industry is only too willing to accommodate this belief.

While the early foundations of franchising were built upon standardization, the success of modern franchising depends on finding ways to meet the ever-changing needs of affluent consumers. New businesses, not even thought of 10 years ago, are sprouting wings and taking to the sky. Franchising organizations capitalize on this era of specialization by expanding through sales to independent parties (who become franchisees) rather than by investing their own money. The capital saved is used by franchisors to develop new and better ways to serve consumers' specialized needs.

Specialization helps franchisees because it creates new marketing niches for franchises to pursue. Offering products and services to those niche customers works for the common good of all in the system. The ongoing trend towards specialization will lead to the creation of new franchises and keep franchising at the forefront of business distribution methods.

UNIFORM SYSTEM

As mentioned earlier, franchising will continue to succeed in the era of specialization by calling upon its traditional roots to see that consumers receive uniform quality—efficiently and cost-effectively—through *uniform systems of operation*. A uniform system brings with it the advantages of mass purchasing power, brand identification, customer loyalty, and capitalizes upon the proven format.

A federal court recently described the importance of uniformity when dealing with a case involving Domino's Pizza:

"The essence of a successful nationwide fast-food chain is product uniformity and consistency. Uniformity benefits franchisees because customers can purchase pizza from any Domino's store and be certain the pizza will taste exactly like the Domino's pizza with which they are familiar. This means that individual franchisees need not build up their own good will. Uniformity also benefits the franchisor. It ensures the brand name will continue to attract and hold customers, increasing franchise fees and royalties."

To serve our mobile society and continue to attract loyal, repeat customers all over the country—and world—franchise systems must utilize uniform systems to provide uniform products and services.

ADVERTISING NETWORK

The term "strength in numbers" aptly describes franchise advertising. Because of collective advertising funds and cooperatives, franchisees—who normally could only afford to advertise locally, if at all—can take advantage of national and regional advertising (which is exorbitantly expensive). Franchisees also benefit from the creative talent that large corporations draw upon to effectively market their products and services. On the other hand, franchisors benefit because they can consolidate their advertising efforts and fund expensive advertising campaigns with the financial help of their franchisees.

Both the national and regional success of a franchise depends largely upon the franchisor's ability to develop name recognition and product or format acceptability. Local, regional and national advertising instills in consumers the confidence that they can go across the country and find—in a franchise outlet—the same quality as they would in their own neighborhood. Advertising networks, therefore, are a vital part of every franchise system.

NAME IDENTIFICATION

Another benefit that potential franchisees can expect is to be identified with the franchisor's name. By delivering a quality service or product (a proven format), and with the help of advertising, franchisors achieve name recognition with the public.

This commodity—recognition—is one of the intangibles that franchisors offer franchisees. As the franchise matures and name recognition increases, this intangible benefit becomes more valuable, and the franchisor often wants to charge new franchisees a higher franchise fee for the privilege of operating under the franchise name.

With a successful franchisor, product or service recognition confers an image of quality, integrity, and trust. Therefore, in addition to obtaining a product or service to sell the public that is presented in a proven format, franchisees also gain instant integrity and recognition. This is one of the reasons franchised businesses seem to enjoy a better track record of success than their non-franchised counterparts. Clearly, with the right franchise system, the new business owner is off to a much better start.

TRAINING

Because reproducing the franchisor's format is so important to the ultimate success of the entire network, many franchisors have strict training requirements. New franchisees are required to attend franchising "universities". Some franchisors use a combination of classroom and on-site training to indoctrinate franchisees in the ways of their systems. This training instills the proven format or methodology in each of its franchisees and gives them some of the knowledge and experience they need. Sharing a proven format with others—so they can replicate it—lies at the heart of franchising. This is the reason why "the simpler the idea the better the franchise".

The training that normally accompanies the sale of a franchise allows people, otherwise inexperienced in the operation of the franchisor's business, to successfully offer the same quality service or product in a uniform manner.

FRANCHISEE NETWORK

For franchisees—especially new ones—the franchise network or "family of franchisees" is an invaluable resource for information and business experience. Because all are working towards a common goal, keen new franchisees can draw freely upon the available knowledge base offered within a franchise structure. "Partnering" with other franchisees can be a great help and, before joining a franchise system, you should consult with some of its franchisees, you'll get valuable inside information (more about this in Chapter 10).

Properly stimulated by the franchisor, the synergy of franchisee relationships can continually spark new methods of operation and product ideas. As new business issues arise, new solutions are reached collectively and every franchisee benefits.

Wise franchisors also draw upon this ready resource. Many improvements to franchise systems have resulted from accepting new ideas and suggestions from their "family of franchisees".

The entire system benefits from the collective knowledge, experiences and mistakes of existing franchisees. This is one of the most valuable and underrated benefits of joining a franchise system.

POWER BUYING AND COMPUTERIZATION

Although not always available, cooperative buying arrangements offered by the franchisor (or franchisee groups), are an important benefit of joining a franchise system. Because some systems use vast amounts of raw materials or ancillary services, volume discounts as well as customized service can be negotiated with vendors. In some industries these discounts or specialized services provide the competitive edge necessary for success. Many franchise systems are also able to help new franchisees with discounts on the initial fixtures and equipment needed to start the business.

A successful franchise system's power buying is an important attribute now that computer equipment has infiltrated almost every aspect of business. Computerization is an expensive capital investment. By working from the franchise system's base of knowledge, franchisees can get help making the correct purchase and maximizing their computers' efficiency. Many franchisors have developed customized software to operate every aspect of the system. Computerized point of sale systems, reservation systems, inventory control, sales report system and data communication between franchisee and franchisor have become standard operating equipment.

Modern franchise systems have developed electronic communication systems for their franchisees. In addition, many franchisors maintain web sites on the Internet and encourage their franchisees to participate in on-line lists (sometimes called "bulletin boards") and/or forums or discussion groups (also called "chat groups"), where common issues and problems are discussed.

Indeed, computerization and purchasing cooperatives are necessities in modern retail and service industries. Few will survive if they do not tele-connect with their suppliers, vendors and customers. In the next century, franchise systems will be propelled forward on this technological surge.

These are the primary building blocks for a successful franchise system and potential franchise buyers should place them at the top of their list of elements to investigate.

2

WHAT IS
A FRANCHISE?

Obvious as this may seem, if you are thinking of buying a franchise, it is important to clearly understand what one is. Unfortunately, the term "franchise" does not lend itself to easy or precise definition. Simply put, it is a method of distributing goods or services, a unique selling concept that fits hand in glove with our highly mobile, service-intensive society.

A BRIEF HISTORY

The booming post-war economy of the 1950's propelled franchising into the modern economic era. The newly-formed interstate highway system provided the infrastructure for new restaurants, hotels and service stations, all designed to meet the changing, growing needs of a new breed of mobile and adventurous Americans. Added to the mix was the power of television which provided the first truly national advertising medium. These dynamic forces, combined with new-found wealth, fueled the franchise fire.

Yet franchising can trace its roots back almost a century from when Isaac Singer first utilized the concept. He reportedly accepted a royalty or license fee from independent salesmen for territorial rights to sell his sewing machine. The invention of the automobile thrust franchising into a higher gear, as it did with many other aspects of American life in the early 1900's. General Motors established dealerships to meet the rising demand for automobiles, and oil companies offered service station franchises to the mechanics of the day, to create an automobile service industry that thrives to this day.

The names Howard Johnson's and Kentucky Fried Chicken could not have been etched into our collective memories without the upsurge of the franchising method of doing business. McDonald's would not have taken on the proportions of an American icon. We owe much to the early franchise pioneers who provided us with a novel business methodology that allowed rapid expansion, the pooling of capital and a harnessing of the American entrepreneurial spirit.

To enlarge on the earlier definition: *franchising is a legal business arrangement, governed and created by a contract, under which the franchisor (owner/supplier) sells to a franchisee (retailer/buyer) the right to sell certain of the supplier's goods and/or services under specific, agreed upon conditions.*

The franchise system benefits both individual franchisees and the franchise as a whole. As described in the last chapter, these benefits usually include:

- proven business format
- standardized method of operation
- national advertising
- franchise name recognition
- franchisee training

- franchisee network
- standardized fixtures and equipment
- professional site location assistance
- centralized buying power
- rules and quality control standards

Franchisors create this system to expand their business without investing more capital or adding personnel and increasing their payroll. In fact, franchisors raise capital by charging franchise fees to their franchisees. In other words, by franchising their products and/or services, franchisors can build both their profits and their business, without spending significant amounts of money.

While most people think of McDonald's, Wendy's, Dunkin' Donuts and Taco Bell as typical franchises, there are also a multitude of car dealerships, hotel chains, convenience stores, service stations, and business and accounting services that operate as franchises also. A closer cousin to franchising, "business opportunity plans" provide the framework for certain dealerships and distributorships that can be easily confused with typical franchises.

Generally speaking, a business opportunity plan is a hybrid of a franchise and a distributor arrangement (though some definitions of "business opportunity plan" do encompass franchises). The most notable differences are that "business opportunity plans" often do not contain the trademark requirement and the laws governing them focus more on specific types of distributorship businesses (such as rack distributors, vending machine routes and video machine sales and placement).

As franchising evolved in the early 1960's, the need for a precise definition increased. But it was not until 1971 that California adopted the first law regulating the sale of a "franchise" and not until the end of the decade that the FTC adopted a regulation on the federal level under the Federal Trade Commission Act. Unfortunately, the definitions adopted by the FTC and California were not identical, and the enforcement structures were very different. These twin starts established a regulatory morass that continues to this day.

There are now three basic approaches used to define a "franchise". The "California model", the "FTC approach" and the "Minnesota model" or "Community of Interest approach". They all require that the purchaser pay a fee and that the buyer receive, in some way, the right to use a trademark, service mark or trade name of the franchisor. From there, the definitions diverge from each other.

THE FTC RULE

This rule requires a franchisee to meet the quality standards of the franchisor. In addition, a franchisor must exert, or have the authority to exert, a significant degree of control over the franchisee's business operation. Finally, the franchisor is required to give "significant assistance" to the franchisee before the relationship is considered a "franchise".

THE CALIFORNIA MODEL

Generally followed by Illinois, Indiana, Maryland, Michigan, North Dakota, Rhode Island, Wisconsin and, with some variances, New York and Virginia, this Model focuses on the franchisor's requirement that a franchisee follow "a prescribed marketing plan".

THE COMMUNITY OF INTEREST APPROACH

Minnesota, Hawaii, South Dakota and Washington follow this approach. Central to it is the requirement that "a community of interest exist between the franchisor and franchisee".

Years of legal interpretation, case law and advisory opinions further define the meaning of many of the esoteric terms and phrases used to define a "franchise". These three main approaches, however, give the average franchise purchaser a good overview of what are generally considered the essential elements of a franchise: payment of an initial franchise fee; the right to use a trademark, service mark or trade name; and an additional ingredient connecting franchisor and franchisee, called either a "marketing plan", "significant assistance" or "community of interest".

3

HOW TO FIND THE RIGHT FRANCHISE FOR *YOU*

The starting point for finding the right franchise is not in any book, nor is it a secret formula. It is so obvious that many would-be franchisees overlook it entirely. It is *you*.

Just as with other aspects of your life, finding the right franchise starts with your interests, background, education and experience. For example: many franchise systems require direct owner involvement in the operation of the business. What kind of business appeals to you? Would you want to manage a restaurant? Do you have the experience or ability to run a computer training facility? Is cleaning carpets going to be a fulfilling enough work experience? Is dealing with folks whose cars are broken-down really your cup of tea?

Before you consider buying a franchise (let alone a specific type of franchise) you should ask yourself some very fundamental questions:

■ How much of a team-player are you?
■ Can you accept direction from others and play the role of follower to get your business rolling?
■ How do you feel about sharing your profits with someone who has not made a direct cash investment in your business?

■ Do you know what it takes to run your own business even under the protection of a franchise system? How many hours are you willing to devote to the business and are you willing to pay the price?

One client, who faced lay-off after 25 years from a major commercial shipping concern (she was the chief shipping clerk, a position of considerable responsibility), was desperate to start her own business. Being inexperienced in new business affairs, she thought franchising could make up any deficit. Although most of her experience involved keeping track of vast amounts of shipments and working on her own with numbers, reports and accounts, she was determined to do "something new" and began looking at temporary employee/personnel placement franchises. She thought working with people would be fun.

Without any professional assistance, she selected a franchise system with a solid background and good track record. Within a year, however, her business was a shambles. When she visited our law offices to lay blame on the franchisor, it became apparent that she, not the franchisor, was at fault. She was absolutely, positively *not* a people-person. She hated dealing with people, had the personality of a snail and just couldn't believe "these people needed so much hand-holding" when she placed them in a position! And the employers were nothing but a bunch of thankless whiners!

The message is clear: before you consider buying a franchise or starting any other business, you should first conduct a thorough self-analysis of your goals, aspirations, abilities (and weak points) and personality traits, good and bad. Be candid with yourself about your level of ability and own up to those traits that are undesirable in a franchisee or any other type of small business owner.

The next step is to consider your interests and knowledge in different business areas. Business advisers the world over routinely advise newcomers to focus on areas where they have an interest. The chances for success are much greater if you choose something you enjoy doing. Few successful people have a strong dislike for their business enterprise.

The value of this self-analysis cannot be overstated. First, know thyself.

WHAT'S YOUR HURRY?

Once you have done a thorough self-analysis, you can start the search for a specific franchise in earnest. You might already have one in mind or simply be exploring franchising in general with the intention of choosing a franchise you believe is right for you. Or, you may be considering starting your own business and simply giving franchising a sideward glance along the way. Whatever your approach, you'll have better results if you do a little "comparison shopping", take the "Consumer Reports approach" to buying a franchise. There are many franchises to choose from in any location or industry.

The first rule is patience. Some people intend to be patient but their juices start flowing at the very thought of starting their own business—"the sooner we get going the better"—they think. Not true. A "no hurry" attitude will serve you best through the entire purchasing process. People who are in a hurry tend to make mistakes and let emotion rule reason. It is important to control your emotions and tell yourself that you have the upper hand. Like our vending machine buyers at the beginning of this book, the majority of people who later regret their franchise purchase decision simply did not take the time to properly shop their purchase at the outset. Sticking to this first rule will allow you to benefit from the information and guidance in this book.

LET THE BUYER BEWARE

The success and resulting growth of franchising are undeniable. It is the preferred choice when compared to business starts that are unsupported by franchising systems. But, while the advantages are obvious and enticing, franchisors and franchisees do fail. Some franchisees, of course, fail of their own accord. Others fail because of a poor franchising system or franchisor malfeasance. Because the franchising concept is being applied to an ever growing number of businesses—some unproven—prospective buyers must proceed cautiously.

We hear mainly of McDonald's, Wendy's, Midas Mufflers and Pizza Hut. No one in the franchising and distribution community likes to talk about the numerous low-investment, ill-managed franchises and business opportunities that sweep the nation each year. Although this happens less frequently today, over-eager entrepreneurs are still taken advantage of by fly-by-night operators. Most victims were driven by emotion rather than prudence, logic and a careful, systematized franchise search.

STARTING YOUR SEARCH

There are a number of resources available to help in your search for the right franchise. To become an astute franchise buyer, you should take advantage of as many of these resources as possible. If you are a computer buff, there is plenty of information on the Internet.

An excellent starting point is the International Franchise Association (IFA), the oldest and largest of the franchise trade associations. While primarily an association of franchise companies, in recent years the IFA has welcomed a large number of franchisees to its ranks. The IFA is fashioning a more balanced approach to their role in the franchising world than in years past and forging a reputation as a moderating voice in the sometimes contentious relationship between franchisors and franchisees. The IFA has a list of publications to assist you with your purchasing decision. Contact:

International Franchise Association
Directory of Membership
1350 New York Avenue N.W.
Washington, DC 20005
(202)628-8000
http://www.franchise.org

The IFA's Web Site includes the IFA's *Franchise Opportunities Online Guide* which contains numerous franchise offerings listed alphabetically, by category and by total cash investment requirements. The IFA Web Site offers an array of information that literally opens a window to the world of franchising—it provides links to other sites such as the Small Business Association Web Site. A bulletin board at the IFA Site offers users a ready exchange of information from around the world.

Two other associations offer information to the franchise purchaser:

The American Association of Franchisees and Dealers
P.O. Box 81887
San Diego, California 92138-1887

(800)773-9858
http://www.aafd.org/
(Recognized by Dow-Jones as a premium franchising site)

and

American Franchisee Association
53 West Jackson Blvd.
Suite 205
Chicago, Illinois 60604
(800) 334-4AFA
http://www.infonews.com/franchise/afa

Both of these franchisee associations provide information to potential franchisees and serve existing franchisee-members by seeking to influence state and federal franchise legislation, developing meaningful dialogue with franchisors concerning the content of franchise agreements, and attempting to bring greater fairness to the franchise relationship. Both associations are dedicated to the plight of franchisees and also maintain a list of publications for the franchise buyer.

The American Association of Franchisees and Dealers' Web page is well worth a visit. In addition to providing information about the Association and tips on buying a franchise, you will find the AAFD Resource Store which offers books, resources, and software all geared to franchisees and franchise buyers.

Pilot Books annually publishes an excellent basic reference titled: "Directory of Franchising Organizations." It lists current U.S. franchises (over 2,200) divided by franchise category, including the necessary investment in each case. For information or to order, contact:

Pilot Books
127 Sterling Avenue
PO Box 2102
Greenport, NY 11944
800-79PILOT
e-mail: feedback@pilotbooks.com

Some offerings on franchising through the popular press
include:

The Franchise Annual: On-line
Info Franchise News, Inc.
728 Center St., P.O. Box 550
Lewiston, N.Y. 14092
(716) 754-4669
http://www.vaxxine.com/franchise/

Entrepreneur Magazine
"Franchise 500 Survey"
(Published in January Edition)
(714) 261-2325
http://www.entrepreneurmag.com

Franchise Update
P.O. Box 20547
San Jose, California 95160-0547
(408) 997-7795
http://www.franchise-update.com

Many of these publications offer a broad range of information and leads to other resources. For instance, Business Resale

Network, a cooperative effort by *Entrepreneur Magazine* and *Franchise Update*, is an online advertising site listing existing franchises for resale. This can be reached by connecting to *Entrepreneur Magazine's* Web Page at http://www.entrepreneur mag.com.

Frandata, a fee-based information resource, gathers information marketed primarily to franchisors and their service-providers and maintains comprehensive information on franchise companies. Frandata has overviews of franchisors within specific industries as well as a multitude of franchisor's disclosure documents (although you can generally obtain the disclosure documents free of charge directly from the franchise company). Frandata can be contacted at:

Frandata
1730 M Street, NW
Suite 800
Washington, D.C. 20036
(202) 659-8640

A few other sites available on the World Wide Web offering information on franchising are:

Franchise Handbook: On-line
http://www.franchise1.com

The American Bar Association's Forum on Franchising
http://www.abanet.org/forums/franchising

Women's Franchise Network
http://www.entremkt.com

Business Start Page
http://www.wp.com/fredfish

With such vast resources available, literally at your finger-tips, there is no reason not to conduct a thorough search for a franchise opportunity. But keep in mind that much of the information given in these publications is industry-oriented. Use these resources, but do not accept any information verbatim. You must always independently investigate the information provided from any source.

As we will talk about in greater detail later in the book, the Federal Trade Commission (FTC) is the only federal agency regulating the franchise industry, their regulation, however, is very loose. The FTC maintains information on franchising in general and may disclose public enforcement actions taken against franchisors.

The Small Business Administration (SBA) has had a growing interest in franchising, offering assistance with loans and general information on franchising. Contact your local SBA office to obtain the information they have available on franchising and the loans they make available to purchase franchises.

In some states, the State Securities Administrator or the Attorney General may have a list of franchise companies registered with the state. Although it is difficult to extract any meaningful information from state and federal officials on specific franchise offerings, they are permitted to disclose publicly-filed actions taken against franchisors. You should seriously consider making the effort to contact these officials to inquire about any actions taken against a franchise company that interests you.

A primary source for information about franchisors may be right around the corner. Assuming that most people would like to own a business in their own community, talking with local franchisees would be the logical place to start when seeking a realistic appraisal. Discussing the system with someone already familiar with it should provide invaluable information.

Other ways you can start your search is to look in the business opportunity section of your local newspaper or attend a franchise trade show. If you do, be very careful and selective. Some franchisors enhance their ads with exaggerated claims while trade shows can be over-hyped, emotionally-charged atmospheres. Many of these "you can't lose" opportunities prove to be exactly the opposite.

The FTC has recently taken action directly against trade show promoters for failing to properly screen and supervise franchise and business opportunity participants. Newspapers and trade show promoters do not insure that the ads or information being distributed are factual. So, especially if this is your initial exposure to franchising, you need to back up all information with hard facts before making any purchasing decision.

Conducting a proper search does not end with choosing the type of franchise you would like to buy, it is only the beginning. While it is important to select an area in which you will be happy, and hopefully successful, remember that patience is the watchword and analysis is imperative. You want to make an intelligent, deliberate decision about how you are going to plot your successful future.

Before you begin your search, it is important to be franchise-educated. Knowing what to look for will clearly improve your selection ability. Your education began the moment you opened this book. Carefully reviewing the remaining chapters will build the foundation of your knowledge. Use your education wisely to eliminate as many risks as possible.

Again, what's your hurry? Whatever your approach, you will have better results by doing a little "comparison shopping"—

taking the 'Consumer Reports' approach to buying a franchise. There are many to choose from, and in virtually every area of possible interest. Remember, the first rule of buying a franchise is patience. The search for the right franchise takes systematic patience—and a systematic plan. Sticking to this first rule will allow you to benefit from the balance of the information and guidance offered in this book.

II

EVALUATING YOUR CHOICES

4

PROTECTION UNDER THE FTC REGULATION AND STATE LAWS

During the late 1960's and early 1970's, a wave of bogus "start your own business" opportunities swept through the United States. Numerous complaints rolled into governmental agencies, prompting state legislatures and the FTC to take action to stop the rash of fraudulent schemes.

It was found that many of the victims were first-time investors who knew little or nothing about purchasing a business. Many lost their life savings or retirement income to fast-talking salespeople who made false claims. The FTC, after reviewing voluminous complaints against these early, fraudulent franchisors, realized that these deceptive and unfair practices occurred largely due to an "informational imbalance" between franchisors and franchise buyers. In light of this, regulators concluded that franchise purchasers should be able to get more complete information about the business system they were going to buy. This gave rise to the disclosure laws in effect today.

To correct the imbalance, the FTC and a number of state governments borrowed the concept of pre-sale disclosure from the securities industry. More precisely, the disclosure and registration policy came about because, under existing securities laws, attempts to prosecute unlawful franchise sellers failed. As a result, it is now standard practice for the proposed buyer to receive disclosure documents in advance of every franchise and business opportunity sale.

The FTC and approximately twenty-five states have adopted laws protecting prospective franchise and business opportunity buyers. In states where no specific state law is on the books, the FTC Rule fills the void. The basic framework of the state laws and the FTC rule is to provide a basic disclosure document prepared by a franchise company to prospective purchasers.

In most instances, the disclosure document sets forth approximately twenty categories of information about the franchise company. This information is vital to your purchasing decision. Although the length of the disclosure document may be somewhat intimidating, take the time to properly review it, this is essential. In the next chapter, we will fully explore what to look for in disclosure documents.

Although the FTC does not require a franchisor to register (file) disclosure documents with that agency, some states—the so-called "registration states"—do require franchisors to file disclosure documents with the State Securities Administrator or the Attorney General. This allows state agencies to regulate franchisors who sell in their states and makes it easy to determine whether a franchisor is complying with the state's law.

If you are buying a franchise in a registration state, your search should begin with a call to the governmental agency in charge of registering franchises, to make sure the franchise company is registered. If it is not, you have reason to be concerned. State registration is a basic requirement of a legitimate franchise sales program and any that does not register is suspect. But remember, not all states require registration.

The following states presently require registration of franchises:

California	New York
Hawaii	North Dakota
Illinois	Rhode Island
Indiana	South Dakota
Maryland	Virginia
Michigan	Washington
Minnesota	Wisconsin

The following states require registration of business opportunity plans:

California	Minnesota
Connecticut	New Hampshire
Florida	North Carolina
Georgia	Oklahoma
Indiana	South Carolina
Iowa	South Dakota
Maine	Texas
Maryland	Utah
Michigan	Washington

While the FTC Rule and various state laws protect prospective franchise buyers, the major drawback is their lack of uniformity. Each state law is slightly different and they all differ from the FTC Rule. Some states require more disclosure information than the FTC Rule; others require less. The FTC Rule states that disclosure in all states must be at least as strict as the FTC Rule. However, if a state chooses to have a tougher regulation than the FTC, that is permitted. Sound confusing? It is. Because of this confusion, it is a good idea to work with an attorney and get—at least—a basic disclosure document from the franchisor.

Again, as a general rule, the important thing to remember is you must find out if the business you intend to buy is a "franchise" or "business opportunity" covered by a protective law. This means the essence of the offering must be analyzed to determine if the proposed relationship will be considered a "franchise" or "business opportunity" under any applicable law. In some locations it may be a "franchise", in others a "business opportunity plan", and still, in others, nothing at all. It all depends upon the applicable definition. As will be discussed later, this may require profesional assistance.

Going back again to our vending machine buyers, one of the pitfalls they fell into was believing that the opportunity they were interested in was not regulated — that is, they did not realize at the time of their purchase that protective laws (in that instance a business opportunity law) required that they receive disclosure documents. Had they understood this, and used it to their advantage, the scam would have been easy to discover.

As a general rule, if you are thinking of starting your own business as a franchisee, don't sign or enter into the transaction until you know that the seller is complying with the various franchise disclosure laws.

If the seller indicates that the company you are considering is not a "franchise" or "business opportunity" under a particular law and you are still interested in entering into a business arrangement, then you are well-advised to seek the services of an attorney. Surprisingly, sellers can sometimes be totally ignorant of the laws protecting franchise and business opportunity buyers. This alone is a sign of inexperience so be on your guard. Information about getting professional assistance is in Chapter 7.

In some states, in addition to disclosure documents and registration requirements, prospective purchasers are given cooling-off periods during which they can cancel a franchise or business opportunity contract *after signing it*. Cooling-off periods are more typically found in business opportunity laws than in franchise laws. It is not a good practice, however, to rely on a cooling-off period in lieu of solid investigation. In other states, franchisors are required to maintain bonding or trust accounts in the state of purchase, and injured purchasers are armed with statutory penalties if the need to initiate legal action should arise. These state and federal laws are a franchisee's Bill of Rights.

In addition to laws regulating the franchise sales, some states also have laws governing a franchisor's termination of or refusal to renew, a franchise. Known as "relationship laws", they prohibit franchisors from terminating or refusing to renew a franchise without "good cause". Franchisees in certain industries, such as service station dealers and automobile dealerships, also have special state and federal laws guarding against unfair terminations. Without these laws, franchisees would have far less protection and fewer rights. In the remaining chapters, we will see how you can use these laws to your advantage.

The following states have franchise relationship laws which may be of assistance at the end of your relationship:

Arkansas	Mississippi
California	Missouri
Connecticut	Missouri
Delaware	New Jersey
Hawaii	South Dakota
Illinois	Virginia
Indiana	Washington
Iowa	Wisconsin
Michigan	Virgin Islands
Minnesota	

Government regulation of franchising and its hybrid, business opportunity plans, can be a confusing maze. Despite the confusion in applying these protection laws, you, the prospective franchise purchaser, should take full advantage of all aspects of the law.

For more specific information concerning the laws which may apply in your situation you may contact the following agencies:

California
Commissioner of Corporations:
Department of Corporations
3700 Wilshire Blvd., Ste. 600
Los Angeles, CA 90010-3001
(213) 736-2741

Connecticut
[Business Opportunity Investment Act]
Securities and Business
Investment Division
Connecticut Department of Banking
260 Constitution Plaza
Hartford, Connecticut 06103
(860) 240-8299

Florida
[Sale of Business Opportunities Act]
Consumer Services Consultant
Department of Agriculture
and Consumer Services
Division of Consumer Services
227 N. Bronough Street
City Centre Bldg., Suite 7200
Tallahassee, Florida 32301
(850) 922-2770
FAX: (850) 487-4177

Hawaii
Securities Examiner
1010 Richards Street
Honolulu, Hawaii 96813
(808) 586-2727

Illinois
Franchise Division
Office of Attorney General
500 South Second Street
Springfield, Illinois 62706
(217) 782-4465

Indiana
Joan Moore Mernitz
Chief Deputy Commissioner
Franchise Section
Indiana Securities Division
Secretary of State
Room E-111
302 West Washington Street
Indianapolis, Indiana 46204
(317) 232-6576

Iowa
[Business Opportunity Promotions Law]
Dennis Britson, Director
Regulated Industries Unit
Department of Commerce
Insurance Division
Securities Bureau
Lucas Building, Second Floor
Des Moines, Iowa 50319

(515) 281-4441
FAX: (515) 281-6467

Kentucky
[Business Opportunity Act]
A. B. Chandler, III
Kentucky Attorney General
1024 Capital Center Drive
P. O. Box 2000
Frankfort, Kentucky 40602-2000
(502) 573-2200

Maryland
Maryland Division of Securities
200 Saint Paul Place,
20th Floor
Baltimore, Maryland 21202-2020
(410) 576-7044

Michigan
Consumer Protection Division
Antitrust and Franchise Unit
Michigan Department of Attorney General
670 Law Building
Lansing, Michigan 48913
(517) 373-7117

Minnesota
Minnesota Department of Commerce
133 East Seventh Street
St. Paul, Minnesota 55101
(612) 296-4026

Nebraska
[Seller-Assisted Marketing Plan Law]
Department of Banking and Finance
1200 N Street
Suite 311
P. O. Box 95006
Lincoln, Nebraska 68509
(402) 471-3445

New York
New York State Department of Law
120 Broadway, 23rd Floor
New York, New York 10271-0332
(212) 416-8211
FAX: (212) 416-8816

North Dakota
Office of Securities
Commissioner
600 East Boulevard, Fifth Floor
Bismarck, North Dakota 58505
(701) 224-4712

Ohio
[Business Opportunity
Purchasers Protection Act]
Ohio Attorney General
30 E. Broad Street
Columbus, Ohio 43215
(614) 466-4320

Oregon
Department of Insurance and Finance
Corporate Securities Section
Labor and Industries Building
Salem, Oregon 97310
(503) 378-4387

Rhode Island
Division of Securities
233 Richmond Street, Suite 232
Providence, Rhode Island 02903
(401) 277-3048

South Dakota
Franchise Administrator
Department of Commerce
Division of Securities
118 West Capital Avenue
Pierre, South Dakota 57501-2017
(605) 773-4823

Texas
[Business Opportunity Act]
Statutory Document Section
Secretary of State
P. O. Box 12887
Austin, Texas 78711
(512) 475-1769

Utah
[Business Opportunity Disclosure Act]
Division of Consumer Protection

Utah Department of Commerce
160 East Three Hundred South
P. O. Box 45804
Salt Lake City, Utah 84145-0804
(801) 530-6701
FAX: (801) 530-6001

Virginia
Chief Examiner
State Corporation Commission
1300 E. Main Street, 9th Floor
Richmond, VA 23219
(804) 371-9671

Washington
Acting Administrator
Department of Financial Institutions
Securities Division
P.O. Box 9033
Olympia, Washington 98507-9033
(302) 902-8760

Wisconsin
Franchise Administrator
Securities and Franchise Registration
Wisconsin Securities Commission
101 E. Wilson Street, Fourth Loor
P.O. Box 1768
Madison, Wisconsin 53701
(608) 266-8559

5

THE DISCLOSURE STATEMENT

Disclosure documents, required under the FTC Rule and most state laws, are the crux of the franchise protection laws. Also known as an Offering Circular, the disclosures contain the ABC's of the opportunity you are exploring and disclose approximately twenty categories of information about the franchisor and the franchise offering. Nothing provides you with more comprehensive information. (See the Appendix for pertinent parts of a sample Offering Circular.)

Although the disclosure approach has not erased all fraudulent franchise offerings, in addition to its other uses, it enables franchise—and business opportunity purchasers—to sort the wheat from the chaff and effectively compare one franchise offering to another. Recent changes in the rules governing the disclosure format used by most franchisors, promise to make the disclosures even more informative and understandable. And learning how to use the disclosure information properly is an important skill for you to acquire at this time.

It is important to mention that *the use of a disclosure document does not mean the government has approved the franchisor or the franchise offering.* Even in states where registration of the Offering Circular is required, the government does not endorse franchise systems. And, the use of an Offering Circular is no guarantee that the contents are truthful or accurate.

Before learning how to use disclosure documents, it is necessary to touch upon whether you will always be able to use this important tool. Not all opportunities to start your own business will technically qualify as legally constituted franchises or business opportunities.

Whether you are—or should be—provided with disclosure documents is determined by state and federal law and lies mainly in the definition of a "franchise" or "business opportunity". The analysis of whether a particular business arrangement is a "franchise" or "business opportunity" can be a complicated one. Because it may require professional assistance, a good practice at the beginning of your search is to *refrain from buying any type of business opportunity unless disclosure documents are provided, or you have received a professional opinion that they are not required.*

If a franchisor or seller of a plan does not voluntarily provide a disclosure document, you have every right to be suspicious. If one is not provided (and you are not scared off) ask for one. If one is not provided in answer to your request, then it might be time to look for another opportunity or seek professional advice. In no event should you pay any money or sign any contracts unless you have been provided with disclosure documents. If there is one thing you should remember from reading this book, it is that *you should always get the disclosure documents!*

Assuming the franchisor or seller has disclosure documents to provide, the next question is *when* are you entitled to receive them. According to the FTC Rule, a franchisor is required to provide disclosure documents at the first personal meeting (that is, a face-to-face meeting), or ten business days before you sign a contract or tender any money to the franchisor, *whichever is sooner.* In other words, if you have a face-to-face meeting with a franchisor more than ten business days before paying any money or entering into a contract, you should be provided with disclosure documents at the time of that first meeting. If, for some reason, you do not have a face-to-face meeting with the franchisor (not a recommended practice) and still want to purchase the franchise or opportunity, the law requires that you be provided with the disclosure documents at least ten business days before entering into a contract or paying any money to a franchisor.

Under many of the state franchise laws, only the ten business day requirement exists. The first personal meeting requirement is found in the FTC Rule. However, because the FTC Rule applies to most franchise or business opportunity type transactions in most states, franchise purchasers may expect disclosure documents to be provided at the time of the first personal meeting if it takes place more than ten business days before the date of purchase.

Most franchise companies, however, routinely provide disclosure documents upon any form of initial contact, whether by mail, phone, on a web-site or in person. Some even pre-screen franchise candidates by mail, requesting qualifying financial and personal background information, before incurring the expense of mailing franchise disclosure documents. It is the unusual situation when disclosure documents are not forthcoming, but when it happens, a franchise purchaser needs to be on highest alert.

Because the disclosures contained in the Offering Circular are so essential to the purpose of the franchise laws (to enable informed buyers to make informed decisions), severe penalties may be imposed on franchise or business opportunity sellers who fail to provide them on time. Federal and state officials may be able to impose fines and, under some state laws, franchise purchasers may rescind the transaction, receiving back their investment and recovering any damage they may have suffered.

Remember that the timing of the presentation of the disclosure documents is important for two reasons: (1) that you be given sufficient time to review the documents (and have an attorney and an accountant review them) before you make your purchasing decision; and (2) that if the disclosures are not presented at the required time, and your opportunity goes sour, you may be able to use this in court to get out of the arrangement and have your money refunded. Obviously, both of these considerations are important.

Continuing briefly with the technicalities of disclosure documents, it should be noted again that in some states the disclosure documents are required to be registered either with the State Attorney General or Securities Administrator. The FTC does not require registration of franchise disclosure documents. To make certain that the franchisor is dealing with you properly, a call to the State Attorney General or Securities Administrator (in those states requiring registration) may be helpful. A list of states requiring registration, along with the addresses and telephone numbers of the various state administrators, appears in the preceding chapter.

If the franchisor is not registered and has dealt with you in a state that requires registration, you can be sure that the Attorney General or Securities Administrator would be most interested in this noncompliance with state law. And, since registration (in selected states) is one of the most basic canons of selling a franchise, a franchisor's failure to register clearly raises a red flag. It is a sure sign that you should proceed with caution. Although failure to register may be an honest oversight, good franchisors seldom fail to register when required.

The registration process has been hailed by some and cursed by others. The concept arose during the heyday of consumerism and, as mentioned before, in response to a wave of fraudulent practices. At the time, franchise registration was viewed as a first defense against franchise sale abuses and, to some degree this has been achieved. But now, in the era of less government, registration is criticized as unnecessary governmental intrusion in the affairs of business.

The primary criticism leveled against the system of franchise registration is its lack of uniformity. Franchisors complain that the system adds to the expense of selling franchises without providing any commensurate benefit to franchise buyers. They believe disclosure alone would provide the essential information and offer less governmental interference.

After adopting stringent franchise registration laws, a few states have backed-off from their original programs. Notably, Michigan and Wisconsin have modified their laws significantly. They still require a limited form of registration, but both states have dropped cumbersome review processes that franchisors believe resulted in unnecessary delays. Most recently, Illinois also eased its law. Whether franchise buyers in these states are in greater jeopardy as a result of the change is yet to be seen. However, an awareness of this trend will keep the future franchise purchaser alert to the shifting sands of franchise regulation.

Disclosure documents must be current. Check the Offering Circular carefully to make certain it has been prepared within the last year. Registration states require annual updates and the FTC format of disclosure calls for information no older than one year. *Never make your purchasing decision on the basis of a disclosure document which is more than one year old.* In addition, franchisors are compelled to disclose material changes during any interim periods. And, although not required, nothing prevents the astute franchise buyer from requesting more up-to-date information when it seems pertinent.

Before you start reading the disclosure documents provided, approach your review with a critical eye . Be prepared to do more than just read. Analyze. Take notes. Develop a system to compare this Offering Circular to others you will review. Be critical. Constantly ask: what will I receive for my investment? What is this company offering that I can't do on my own? Also question the truth of what you read. Although disclosure documents are required to be accurate, keep in mind that they are also a marketing tool for the franchise company. Even with the tight requirements of the mandated disclosure formats, there is room for marketing exaggerations.

Do not make the mistake of believing that the disclosures are accurate just because the federal or state governments require them or because the franchise company is registered with a particular state. In fact, many states and the FTC require a disclaimer be placed on the cover sheet of the Offering Circular indicating that it has NOT been reviewed by governmental agencies and that you should not take the requirement of registration or disclosure to mean that it has been reviewed.

State franchise examiners concentrate mainly on technical compliance with their state law's requirements rather than conducting a "background check" on the franchisor and its officers. And, they do very little to determine if the contents of the Offering Circular are accurate. Unless the franchise company has become known in another state for past fraudulent activities, an examiner is unlikely to uncover the bad apples.

The statements and representations made in the disclosure documents are required by law to be accurate and fully disclose the material terms of all issues affecting your purchase. Nevertheless, it is sometimes difficult to test the accuracy of the statements despite a thorough investigation of the company and the franchise opportunity. Unfortunately, sometimes it is not until after the purchase that the misrepresentations or inaccuracies surface. While it is sometimes difficult to prevent this, a careful investigation will usually reveal some telltale signs. Staying vigilant and maintaining a healthy skepticism will help you avoid a fatal mistake.

Becoming familiar with the general structure of the Offering Circular (disclosure document) will help you analyze the disclosures. Most disclosure documents are set up the same way. They must have a table of contents, approximately twenty-two disclosure items and a number of attachments. The attachments should include a copy of the franchise agreement you will be required to sign as well as any ancillary agreements, financial statements regarding the franchisor's net worth and a list of all franchisees. For examples of key sections of an Offering Circular and a typical franchise agreement, see the Appendix.

There are two basic disclosure formats used by franchisors: The FTC format and the Uniform Franchise Offering Circular format. The Uniform Franchise Offering Circular (UFOC) is the most widely used franchise disclosure format. Developed by the North American Securities Administrators' Association in the mid-1970's, the UFOC format is generally accepted by most states and the FTC (the FTC allows the UFOC format to be used in lieu of the FTC format). In fact, the UFOC format has become so widely accepted by the registration states that the FTC format has fallen into disfavor and is rarely used. Because most, if not all, Offering Circulars you will see will be prepared under the UFOC format, most of the comments and examples that follow will focus on the UFOC format. The sample Offering Circular sections in the Appendix were prepared in the UFOC format.

Although you may be intimidated by the length of the franchise disclosure documents, reading them from cover-to-cover is an absolute must. You must ask yourself at this point: *If I am not willing to read and digest this information, should I be running a new business?* This is a question only you can answer. It is important for you to understand the disclosure documents and the franchise agreement, the nature of the business, the duties imposed on you and the franchisor, so you can discuss it intelligently with your attorney or professional advisor. So, if you are asking yourself if you should read all of this, the answer is an unequivocal "YES".

Thanks to the North American Securities Administrators Association (NASAA), the UFOC is now easier to read. The 1993 revisions to the UFOC Guidelines stipulated that Offering Circulars must now be prepared in "plain English". All legal antiques like "whereas", "hereinafter", and "including but not limited to" have been banished. In addition, NASAA has prescribed the use of tables and charts instead of lengthy and confusing dissertations on the legalities of the franchise agreement. NASAA's effort was to produce a leaner but more informative Offering Circular. See Items 6, 7, 9 and 17 of the sample UFOC in the Appendix for examples of information presented in chart and table formats. The "plain English" format, however, requires that you carefully and thoroughly read the franchise agreement itself.

Now that you are ready to read the Offering Circular, let's review some of the basic elements. As you look over the Table of Contents you will see a number of important items which should attract your attention. The labels themselves should alert you to them. A typical Table of Contents found in a Uniform Franchise Offering Circular is as follows:

ITEM 1   The Franchisor, Its Predecessors and Affiliates
ITEM 2   Business Experience
ITEM 3   Litigation
ITEM 4   Bankruptcy
ITEM 5   Initial Franchise Fee
ITEM 6   Other Fees

ITEM 7	Initial Investment
ITEM 8	Restrictions on Sources of Products and Services
ITEM 9	Franchisee's Obligations
ITEM 10	Financing
ITEM 11	Franchisor's Obligations
ITEM 12	Territory
ITEM 13	Trademarks
ITEM 14	Patents, Copyrights and Proprietary Information
ITEM 15	Obligation to Participate in the Actual Operation of the Franchise Business
ITEM 16	Restrictions on What the Franchisee May Sell
ITEM 17	Renewal, Termination, Transfer and Dispute Resolution
ITEM 18	Public Figures
ITEM 19	Earnings Claims
ITEM 20	List of Outlets
ITEM 21	Financial Statements
ITEM 22	Contracts
ITEM 23	Receipt

Item 1 addresses the background of the franchise company. Although Chapter 9 is devoted exclusively to this topic, here is where you can begin to evaluate the stability of the franchisor and one of the most important attributes to review. Ask yourself:

■ How long has the company been in operation?
■ Did the founders initially run a business that spawned the franchising network?
■ Have there been any predecessor companies and why were changes made?
■ What affiliated companies exist and what purpose do they serve in relation to the franchise operation?
■ How long has the company offered franchises?

The answer to these questions can usually be found in these important first few pages of the document. Note any unanswered questions and be sure to get the answers.

The information in Item 2 allows you to continue your analysis of the company's stability. Here, you will find information on the officers and directors, and a general idea of how stable the franchise organization is. Although the UFOC format calls for only five years of background information on the officers and directors, it will provide the essence of their work history and allow you to gauge the stability of the core group of executives. These are the people you are trusting with your business future—check them out—make sure you are satisfied with their experience and length of service with the company. Again, do not blindly accept everything you read. You must conduct a critical review to protect your interests.

Items 3 and 4, disclosing the litigation and bankruptcy history of the franchisor and its principal officers, must be thoroughly reviewed. Of course, the shorter the disclosures in this area the better. A long bankruptcy history is not a positive sign. On the other hand, disclosed litigation, while an important item to review, does not necessarily indicate instability. It may, however, indicate other problems in the franchise system. The reason litigation, in and of itself, is not always a negative sign is that, unfortunately, operating a franchise system spawns disagreement and, sometimes, disputes. Not everyone is successful and not all franchisees are golden. Franchise litigation can be a two-way street. Look over this item carefully to understand the nature of the dispute before jumping to any conclusions.

Contacting the involved franchisee can be an eye opener. They may be willing to tell you things about the franchisor you won't learn elsewhere. But, before you write off the franchisor, keep in mind that there are generally two sides to a story; the franchisor should be given equal time to respond to the disgruntled franchisee's perception of events.

An expanded discussion of the first four UFOC Items appears in the next chapter.

Items 5, 6 and 7 give information on the franchise fee, start-up costs and other related costs. In essence, these three items will tell you what your total investment will be. Although this is a good place to start assessing your financial commitment (and recent improvements to the UFOC provide more detail than in the past), you should continue to investigate this aspect of your franchise investment throughout your search. Questioning existing franchisees, especially the more recent ones, is a good way to check the franchisor's estimates of costs. This is obviously an important area and the point where you need to re-evaluate your financial resources to make sure you have the appropriate capital to begin your venture.

The franchise fee is the first item you will encounter. Most franchise companies charge an initial fee for your franchise rights. The fee is primarily to compensate the franchisor for its expenses, costs and the sale of its experience and know-how. The savvy franchise purchaser will compare one franchisor's franchise fee to another's and assess the value of any difference. Focus mainly on the overall investment and the projected return. If you think about the franchise fee from your point of view as a prospective franchisee, it is the fee you pay for the privilege of doing business under a certain name and style for a period of years. In determining whether or not the fee is reasonable, think about how many years it will take to earn it back out of your profits. Your accountant, if experienced in the franchise field, can give you rules of thumb about how long it should take to amortize a franchise fee.

In addition to the franchise fee, the franchisor should disclose estimates for rent or real estate costs, insurance requirements and costs, construction or build-out costs, start-up inventory and other related expenditures to set up your operation. Another area for comparison is the ongoing royalty fee. Most franchise companies charge a continuing fee, payable weekly or monthly, which is generally based on some percentage of gross sales or revenue. It is important to study these fees carefully since they all come off the bottom line.

As is the case with any new venture, one of the common pitfalls is underestimating the amount of capital necessary to begin your business. One of the perceived benefits of purchasing a franchise is drawing on the experience of others in order to avoid pitfalls. And, to some degree, this is true in the area of your initial investment. Keep in mind however, that, except for those fees paid directly to the company, franchisors give you estimates of costs and expenses for all items. Each locale and location is different so be ready to adjust your bottom line to account for local requirements and increases. *It is a good idea to overestimate your operating expenses. Give yourself a cushion, at least for the first year.*

The disclosure documents should also explain in great detail the obligations imposed upon the franchisor as well as those imposed upon you, the franchisee. It is customary to set forth these obligations in separate provisions (Items 9 and 11). Some typical obligations imposed on the franchisor include:

- training
- help finding a location
- ongoing consultation to help you in the operation beyond the initial stages
- duty to protect the integrity of the trademark
- supplying any necessary products or pertinent services
- providing sales manuals and aids
- coordination of regional and/or national advertising

TRAINING

As mentioned in the initial chapter, training is one of the essential reasons for joining a franchise system. Items 9 and 11 both discuss training, with Item 9 talking about training from the franchisee's viewpoint:

- what is required in terms of mandatory or voluntary attendance
- whether the franchisee bears any additional cost
- the length of the training program
- where it is conducted

Item 11 tells you about the franchisor's training obligations. While some of the information duplicates that in Item 9, additional information is provided. Look for the names, experience and background of the franchisor's training personnel and a complete outline of the training program. (Some franchisors set out detailed training information in an exhibit to the Offering Circular—the sample UFOC in the Appendix reflects this practice.) The training outline is required to set out the subjects covered, where they are taught (classroom or on-the-job) and the time devoted to each subject. Study these sections of the UFOC carefully and inquire further if you are unclear about anything to do with the training program. If possible, find out if any training classes are in progress during your visit and whether you can briefly attend a class. This firsthand experience may pay great dividends.

As we will discuss later, the training program is your first opportunity beyond the sales experience to begin evaluating the franchisor's performance. A training disaster is an ominous sign. Use the tools provided to assess the quality of the training program in advance of your purchase—the quality of the training program is your window on the future performance of the franchise system.

In addition to mandatory training, other requirements imposed upon the franchisee may include:

- monthly accounting to the franchisor
- payment of royalties
- contribution to advertising funds
- operating in accordance with the franchisor's manual
- maintaining certain business hours, and, in certain situations
- an obligation to take on new products or provide additional services as dictated by the franchisor

It is important for you to understand what the franchisor promises to do and, more importantly, not do. Franchise agreements can be craftily worded so that future help from the franchisor is mentioned but not required. This type of quasi-promise is usually stated as: "Franchisor *may* provide support services as it deems necessary." Take time to distinguish between the "shall" and "may" clauses. It will result in a much better understanding of what the franchisor is committed to do. To study this further review both the sample UFOC and Franchise Agreement in the Appendix—note that UFOC Items 9 and 11 cross-reference corresponding sections of the Franchise Agreement.

Equally important is understanding what is required of you. A clear picture of these obligations from the outset will work to avoid misunderstandings and mis-communications as your relationship with the franchisor develops. Unfortunately, many franchisees simply overlook some of the responsibilities imposed on their side of the bargain.

Some of the other information you will—or should—find in the disclosure documents, will include the franchisor's policy on renewal, termination, trademark and patent ownership, and a variety of other topics. Determine which areas are most important and begin to consider whether negotiation is necessary. Item 13 discusses the trademarks, service marks and trade names of a franchisor which the franchisee will be licensed to use. Think of the Golden Arches and the little Wendy's girl in pigtails and you'll realize how important a trademark is to a franchise system. The systems' trademarks embody all of its good will, uniform quality and advertising effort.

With less well-known systems which are still building their trademark image, it is very important to make sure the marks are properly registered with state and federal trademark offices. From the franchisee's viewpoint, it is crucial that the franchisor have its trademarks and service marks registered with the United States Patent and Trademark Office upon the Principal Register. If the franchisor has not obtained this essential trademark protection and status, the system has not taken the steps needed to protect their marks. This could ultimately render your license to use the marks useless since outsiders may lay claim to a prior use of the trademark and prevent the franchise system from continuing to use the marks.

Also review Item 13 to determine if any challenge to the franchisor's marks exists. If a third party claims an earlier superior right and openly challenges the franchisor's rights to the marks, this must be disclosed. Naturally, if the dispute is resolved in favor of the third party, the system's identifying trademarks could be stripped away. Analyzing the status of the franchisor's trademarks and any challenges to the marks is one area where professional assistance is essential. Do not overlook this crucial area of your franchise purchase.

A number of important attachments should accompany the disclosure documents. The three main items are audited financial statements of the franchisor's corporation or business organization, the franchise agreement you will be required to sign, and a list of franchisees within the franchisor's system. Each attachment is worthy of careful study. The sample UFOC in the Appendix references all of these attachments and the Appendix contains a sample of the most essential clauses of a Franchise Agreement.

The financial statements should be reviewed by an accountant to determine their accuracy and give you a financial picture of the franchisor's stability. The financial statements must be audited and the UFOC guidelines require franchisors to provide the last 2-3 years of statements. The audit requirement means the statements must bear the signature and approval of a certified public accountant who is placing his or her own professional liability on the line. Only interim financial statements (those produced between fiscal years) are permitted to be unaudited.

Even if your eyes glaze over when confronted with endless columns of numbers, financial statements can be a reliable source of additional information not required in the narrative portion of the UFOC. *Remember, because they are audited by certified public accountants—disinterested third party professionals with licenses to protect—audited financial statements are presumed to be more reliable than those that are unaudited.*

First, read the auditor's or accountant's cover statement (called the Auditor's Report). Usually one page, the report tells you whether the accountant is providing an unqualified endorsement of what the financial statements purport to represent or whether issues have arisen during the audit requiring him or her to withhold that opinion. The auditor's opinion must be issued in accordance with "generally accepted accounting principles", or "GAAP" for short. These principles are established by the accounting profession to guide all accountants when rendering opinions and employing accepted methodology.

The rules established under GAAP differ from the guidelines governing the creation of the UFOC document. Because of this, different categories of information are dealt with under each set of rules. For instance, non-franchise litigation may be disclosed in the financial statements but not in the Item 3 Litigation section of the UFOC. So use the financial statements to uncover additional information.

Another area of the financial statements which should be explored is the "Notes" section which expand on and explain certain numerical entries. Auditors add notes in situations where they do not want readers to be misled or where they feel that some further explanation is required. Normally, the "blemishes" (those items that the company would prefer not to discuss) are found in the Notes section. Special arrangements between the officers/owners and the company itself are revealed and significant litigation that the auditors think may create unknown financial risks is disclosed. Reading past the incomprehensible numbers may pay large dividends.

Although not required, the franchisor's financial statements might separate out the financial results for company-owned franchise units (if any). This item deserves scrutiny and may be the only information in the UFOC regarding the income potential of the unit you are thinking of buying.

The two other attachments, the franchise agreement and the list of franchisees, will be discussed in separate chapters.

The importance of obtaining disclosure documents, making certain they are current, and reviewing them with professional assistance cannot be over-emphasized. Remember, this may be your only chance to thoroughly explore before investing a substantial sum.

Many of the remaining chapters build upon the information contained in the disclosure documents and provide the foundation upon which you should base your buying decision.

6

FINANCIAL FEASIBILITY

Once you have found a franchise (or more than one) that seems promising, and looked over the disclosure documents, it is time to address the central issue of whether the proposed investment is worthwhile in economic terms. When evaluating a franchise investment, it is extremely important to test its financial possibilities by formulating financial projections for at least the first few years of ownership.

Set up a spreadsheet analysis of cash flow for a period of three years starting on the date you estimate your new business will open. This is not as difficult as it may sound and is similar to setting up a household budget. See Table 1—CASH FLOW PROJECTIONS for a sample form.

Table 1 CASH FLOW PROJECTIONS

	Year 1	Year 2	Year 3
INCOME			
revenue from sales			
revenue from services			
other revenue			
Total Revenue			
(Cost of Goods Sold)			
GROSS PROFIT			
EXPENSES			
Selling Expenses			
shipping			
advertising			
miscellaneous			
Total Selling Expenses			
Franchise Expenses			
franchise fee			
advertising fees			
royalties			
franchisee association			
Total Franchise Expenses			
Operating Expenses			
rent			
payroll			
payroll tax			
disability insurance			
workers' compensation			
office supplies			
computer support			
telephone			
utilities			
postage			
equipment rental			
travel/entertainment			
cleaning service			
property & casualty insurance			
accounting/bookkeeping			
miscellaneous			
Total Operating Expenses			
TOTAL EXPENSES			
NET CASH FLOW			

Enter the expenses on your spreadsheet by using the costs and expenses provided by the franchisor in items 5, 6 and 7 of the UFOC. *If, however, the numbers provided are only the franchisor's estimates of costs that will be payable to others, you should do your own research and make any necessary modification.* For example, the franchisor may provide an estimate for rent based on the average rents for its franchise units across the country, but if you are thinking of buying a unit in a major metropolitan area, the rent will probably be higher. Also, don't forget that costs of operation will rise each year with the rate of inflation, *so estimates for the second and third year should reflect those increases.* You can find out other costs by simply making a few phone calls, e.g., an insurance broker will tell you the approximate annual cost of property and casualty, workers' compensation and disability insurance and the local utilities will give you fairly accurate estimates of their costs based on the amount of space you are projected to occupy.

The only way to project "Revenues", or how much money you expect your franchise to bring in, would be to question existing franchisees (see Chapter 10 Investigating Existing Franchisees) and to take into account any "earnings claims" (see Chapter 11, Earnings Claims) made by the franchisor, carefully evaluating the franchisor's presentation of the facts and assumptions underlying such earnings claims.

In formulating your projections, you will find it necessary to assume that certain facts are true, for the purpose of your analysis. The rule on such assumptions is that they be as "reasonable" as possible under the circumstances. Many businesspeople and accountants prefer to prepare three sets of cash flow projections, a "best case" scenario, a "worst case" scenario and an "expected case" scenario. In this way, one can analyze the results based on differing sets of assumptions. For example, if your unit must be built and fixtured before opening, the results of your projections may differ substantially if you open when expected or two months later than expected. By examining the results under these three different sets of assumptions, one gets a fuller picture of the "disaster" and the "home run", as well as the likeliest result based on current information.

After you finish, discuss the projections you prepared with your accountant (see Chapter 7, Professional Assistance). An experienced accountant can often tell you how reasonable or unreasonable your assumptions are and can provide a wealth of information regarding expected income and expenses. He or she can also tell you whether the franchise fee is reasonable and, most important, whether the return on your investment will be enough given the risk and labor involved.

TERRITORIAL LIMITATIONS AND DEMOGRAPHIC RESEARCH

Franchise offerings are typically limited to a geographical area; a county, city, town or, for the more mature franchises, a circular area with a diameter measured in miles or city blocks. For example, you pay a franchise fee for the right to do business as the only McDonald's unit in Smallville. This brings up several issues:

1. Does Smallville have a large enough consumer population to support a McDonald's?
2. How many McDonald's units compete for business in the greater area surrounding Smallville, and is there enough population in this greater area to support them all?
3. Is Smallville a growing area in terms of consumer population?
4. Can you identify demographic trends which will tend to increase or decrease future business (e.g., more two-income families in an area tends to increase eating out at fast food restaurants)?

These types of issues may be researched. Many towns and counties maintain Internet web sites with loads of information on their areas and facilities. The United States Department of Commerce site has census information regarding most counties in the United States and many state and other governmental agencies will supply demographic information on smaller territories. By examining past rates of growth in population and competitive businesses, you can project growth rates into the future. Remember that although you will be a part of a national franchise enterprise, your own business and livelihood will be local. So it is important to do a thorough inspection of the area, identify the competition (both your fellow franchisees and outside competing businesses) and find out as much about them as possible.

VISIT THE FRANCHISOR

After you read the disclosure materials and do your financial and demographic analyses, if you are still interested in the proposed purchase, it is prudent to schedule a lengthy visit to the franchisor's business headquarters. The franchisor is not only selling you a business; it is also the leader of the franchise "family" you are interested in joining. The health and future of the franchisor is of prime concern to you. Spend at least two days visiting, at a time when you can speak to all of the officers, particularly the chief executive officer, the chief financial officer and the heads of operations, marketing and advertising. The CEO is the person with the strategic vision for the future of the company while the CFO is in charge of the company's financial infrastructure. The heads of operations, marketing and advertising are in charge of those areas that are most important to franchisees. Engage them in conversation and take the opportunity to ask any questions that remain unanswered.

As previously stated, it is a good idea to attend a training program in order to better assess its effectiveness because the quality of the training program is your window on the future performance of the franchise system.

Keep in mind during your visit that this is the team you may want to join. Try to assess whether the franchisor's goals are to build a business over the long term or simply to sell as many units as possible, and whether the various members of the team will help your business flourish.

7

PROFESSIONAL ASSISTANCE

The sooner new franchise buyers realize they are in unfamiliar, uncharted territory, the better off they are. Professional assistance is so important that the cover page of the FTC disclosure document contains the following recommendation:

> READ ALL OF YOUR CONTRACT CAREFULLY. BUYING A FRANCHISE IS A COMPLICATED INVESTMENT. TAKE YOUR TIME TO DECIDE. *IF POSSIBLE, SHOW YOUR CONTRACT AND THIS INFORMATION TO AN ADVISOR, LIKE A LAWYER OR AN ACCOUNTANT.* IF YOU FIND ANYTHING YOU THINK MAY BE WRONG OR ANYTHING IMPORTANT THAT HAS BEEN LEFT OUT, YOU SHOULD LET US KNOW ABOUT IT. IT MAY BE AGAINST THE LAW.

We strongly recommend that you heed this advice. Here are some reasons why:

■ The FTC studied the franchise sales process for many years. It concluded that many inexperienced franchise investors would have avoided financial ruin if they had the benefit of professional assistance and guidance. Do not make the same mistake as these early franchise purchasers.

- Buying a franchise may well be the most important decision you ever make. Trying and failing is one thing, but investing in a bad business proposition is simply foolish.

- In proportion to your overall investment and the risk of starting a new business, the cost of professional assistance is minimal.

- Starting your own business can be a highly emotional experience. If you are excited and eager to begin, you may overlook some of the pitfalls and negative aspects of the franchise you wish to purchase. This is where a lawyer and quite possibly an accountant come into the picture.

- Buying a franchise is often not more than buying a concept. The concept may appear good in theory but *the concept is only as good as the franchisor*. To properly evaluate the franchisor and the financial information provided to you, the help of a lawyer and an accountant may be indispensable.

- The franchisor has certainly used a lawyer and an accountant to put the plan together. This alone should be enough to alert you that you need the same type of professional assistance.

- Professional assistance will help guide you through the confusing, complex maze of state and federal franchise laws as well as complicated disclosure documents and contractual provisions.

- The disclosure document and franchise agreement you receive from a franchisor may each range anywhere from thirty to fifty pages. The uninitiated franchise-investor will not be able to properly analyze all of the information provided.

- Ethical franchisors will advise you to obtain the services of an attorney and an accountant, while others are more interested in sales than your well-being and would prefer that you simply sign the document on their terms (which you should never do without getting professional help).

- Working with an attorney (and/or accountant) may enhance

your bargaining position with the franchisor. Quite possibly, with professional assistance, you may be able to negotiate a better deal with the franchisor and recapture the cost of the professional fees.

You should hire an experienced franchise attorney to review the disclosure documents, the applicable state and federal laws, and the franchise agreement. An accountant should review the financial statements accompanying the disclosure documents. You might also want to get an accountant's advice about financing and your business plan if you intend to borrow money from a bank to start your new venture.

An experienced accountant can give you practical advice on what to expect financially as a franchisee: anticipated rates of return on investment; whether the franchise fee and the length of the franchise term are reasonable; and other business issues. An accountant is also needed on an ongoing basis to deal with the myriad of federal, state and local taxes; payroll deductions for unemployment and disability; and the preparation of annual financial statements.

Remember, entering into a relationship with a franchisor is like taking on a new partner or entering into a marriage. You should try to get to know your partner as much as possible before you leap into the decision. With professional assistance *before* you buy a franchise, the likelihood of failure is diminished.

WHERE TO FIND THE HELP YOU NEED

Finding the *right* attorney and accountant for your franchising search—and ongoing operation—is important. You wouldn't go to a general practitioner for a heart transplant and you shouldn't use the lawyer who did your divorce to help you enter into a complicated business transaction. Legal practice in the securities or franchise area is highly specialized.

The American Bar Association's Forum on Franchising is a special committee of attorneys that regularly practice in the franchising field. The Forum on Franchising conducts sophisticated seminars attended mainly by lawyers who devote their practices to franchising and distribution law matters in order to keep current on all of the latest legal trends and issues confronting franchisors and franchisees. The Forum publishes a list of its members which is geographically indexed. Using a Forum lawyer will put you in touch with the "heart transplant specialist" of the franchise legal world.

For the latest copy of the directory, write or contact the Forum on Franchising staff at:

American Bar Association Forum on Franchising
ABA Service Center
(800)285-2221
http://www.abanet.org/forums/franchising/home.html

To find an accountant, ask other franchisees for a recommendation. (Accountants often specialize in a given business activity so your best sources of referral are others in the same business.)

If you do not have an existing relationship with a lawyer and/or accountant, some of these tips may be of help:

- If you know a lawyer who is not experienced in the franchise field, ask him or her to recommend a lawyer who is.
- Or, if you know an accountant but not a lawyer—or vice versa —ask for a professional referral. This is often the best way to get to the right person.

Once you receive the correct referrals:

- Set an appointment before you begin the selection process, the advisors may have additional investigatory aids or guidelines for you to follow. In addition, they may have some experience with or background information on the specific franchise opportunities that you intend to pursue.

- During the initial meeting, make sure you get a clear explanation of the professional service to be rendered as well as the fees that will be charged for the service. Ask for a written fee agreement.

- Always follow your advisors' guidelines. But do not overlook the need to control certain aspects of the professional relationship (and keep down the legal and accounting fees) by first doing your homework. For example, you may want to establish an efficient procedure as to when to bring disclosure documents in for review, what to do in advance of the professional review etc.

- If you select a few franchise areas that are of interest, carefully review each offering circular and franchise agreement before you submit it to your advisor for review. As you review, jot down your areas of concern and give them to your advisor so that he or she may keep them in mind during their review.

- When your advisor has finished the review, be prepared to discuss the documents, why the franchise interests you, why you believe this may be the right one for you, etcetera.

Remember that the professional is there to *advise* not decide for you. While your lawyer will provide valuable legal and business advice, the final decision is yours and you must be prepared to make it. After weighing all of the pluses and minuses, select the franchise that offers the best deal, suits your background, is affordable and offers the kind of help you want.

When you are planning to spend thousands of dollars on a franchise, working with a lawyer and accountant is an indispensable part of the transaction. Choosing the right team and using them wisely and efficiently is equally important. But keep in mind that only *you* can select the franchise that is right for you.

8

FRANCHISE
SALESPEOPLE
AND BROKERS

Selling a franchising concept is similar to selling any other product or service. Franchisors use their own salespeople and business brokerage firms to sell their franchises nationally and your first encounter with the franchisor might be through a salesperson or broker. Keep in mind that they are "sales" people, hired or commissioned by the franchisor. Just like any other salesperson, their job is to "persuade" you to buy what they're selling. You may hear a lot of sales talk and an emotional pitch designed to encourage you to get started in your own business immediately. *If this happens, be careful: overselling a franchise concept may signal a weak system, one that is desperate to sell franchises to anyone with a heartbeat.*

The best franchises sell themselves. Sales people offering the better systems will want you to thoroughly investigate the offering and compare it the competition. Look for these signals. If they are not present, perhaps you need to look elsewhere.

Many sales people are well versed in the art of flattery, telling you that you are a great entrepreneur, that you have the "right stuff", and that the sooner you get started the more money you will make. *The information provided in these sales presentations is the least important you will obtain during the entire sales process. It is sales talk.* The hard core information upon which you should base your purchase is found in the disclosure documents, the professional evaluation from your attorney and accountant, and your own investigation of the franchisor's network.

This is the time when it's especially important to remember the self-analysis you originally conducted. Remind yourself of your strengths and weaknesses, your likes and dislikes—they will usually ring truer than the comments of someone you just met. Also keep your systematized game plan in mind. It is easy to grow too eager too early and make the wrong decision. You need to consider all of the options and take your time about it.

This is not to say that all sales people, brokers or business brokerage firms are unprofessional or will mislead you. Just be aware that these are people with much to gain from making a sale. Many are on commission and may receive part of the franchise fee. But, once the franchise is sold, they probably will have little to no involvement in the system's performance. As a result, most salespeople or brokers will have little incentive to make sure that promises are kept. And some may exaggerate and possibly misrepresent information, which is not permitted under the law.

For example, the first thing you want to know—and the first thing sales people want to tell you—is how much you are going to earn if you buy a particular franchise. This is obviously significant information and you should never take the sales person's word for what you can expect to earn…insist on proper documentation. *"Earnings claims" must be substantiated with documentation taken from existing franchises or some other reliable financial source.* A sales person who tells a franchise buyer how much money he or she can expect to earn operating a franchise, without having any reasonable basis and *without providing proper sub-*

stantiating documentation in a disclosure document, is engaging in an outright unlawful practice.

Know the people you are dealing with and understand their motivation. This will serve you well as you continue to analyze new franchise opportunities.

Finally, any verbal promises made outside of the franchise agreement are generally not enforceable, so any representation you rely upon should be put into writing and included in the franchise agreement. In other words: *if you want to be able to make a franchisor keep a promise, make sure it is written into the franchise agreement.*

9

THE HISTORY OF THE FRANCHISOR

Franchising has earned a solid reputation in the business world because of certain well run, highly sophisticated franchise systems popular with the American people. Generally speaking, the reason these franchises are successful is the total commitment of the franchisor to the excellence of the product or service and the success of its franchisees. Franchisors with a solid history and background are successful...those with the success of the franchisee at the cornerstone of their systems have excelled beyond their own expectations.

On the other hand, many of franchising's biggest disasters have occurred when franchisors put quick riches ahead of long term growth and stability. A real life example underscores the point.

A few years ago a new franchise opportunity was offered in the mid-west. It was a novel concept that intended to capitalize on the auto-racing craze. We'll just call it "The Loser's Circle". It started from a single store that offered all sorts of auto-racing paraphernalia. The franchise idea was rolled-out to auto-racing fans, and was even marketed at some of racing's premier events. The prospects looked good and avid race fans saw its potential.

A minimal and inadequate Offering Circular was distributed by the franchisor. Unfortunately, because of their lack of experience, most of the buyers did not know how minimal and inadequate. But there was one item that should have caught their attention—a short company history with no actual experience in operating any of the stores, let alone a franchise system.

A quick review by an experienced eye revealed that the franchising company had just been formed within the last year. It had no audited financial statements because of its brief history, and the officers and directors had varied experiences, none of which had anything to do with "The Loser's Circle" stores. The list of franchisees contained only 2 names. The "flagship store", located in a nearby city, had operated for only a brief time and doubled as the warehousing operation for the "system".

As it turns out, the flagship store was the original store in the system but things were not quite as they appeared. The store was started by someone with a bright idea but no capital or ability to expand. Enter the "franchisor", a company from out west that looked for "great new retail concepts" and tried to turn them into franchises. "The Loser's Circle" was not their only venture. They had a habit of bouncing from one doomed franchise concept to another. Some of this was even alluded to in the Offering Circular—but no one understood what it meant.

The flagship store, it was later learned, was not part of the franchise system at all, but independently-owned by the originator. He had authorized the "franchisor" to use the name and the concept. The originator, in turn, agreed to help the franchisees obtain their initial and ongoing inventory. The franchisor did not operate any of the stores for a single day. Shortly after the buyers paid their money, the originator's supplier went out of business. Since the franchisor had no operating experience, a substitute inventory supplier could not be found and the end was near.

The franchising company, nothing more than a telephone number in a western city, was gone before anyone could blink. Although the officers and directors were chased by state and federal regulators, the group of would-be franchisees never recovered a nickel.

This sad tale has, unfortunately, been repeated throughout the history of franchising. Be on guard—learn how to investigate the franchisor's history before you become an esteemed member of "The Loser's Circle".

A franchisor's history normally starts with the concept it created and operated as an independent business before franchising and developing a system based on its experience. The success of the more established, household-name franchise systems has turned these companies into massive corporate entities generally far removed from their founders. But, almost each one of these popular, successful systems began as a single independent unit that struggled to expand beyond its humble beginnings. Ray Kroc, the founder of McDonald's, Harlan Sanders (Kentucky Fried Chicken), and Dave Thomas (Wendy's) all started this way.

Look for this connection to the founders. If the company has achieved great success, make sure the system has kept the philosophy of its founders. Do the corporate "suits" articulate a connection to the original commitment and pride that made the system successful? What does the organization do to keep in touch with the "rank and file" franchisee?

With a new, start-up franchise system, make sure the sellers of the plan are the founders of the original concept. Some companies are in the business of finding new retail concepts, getting a license agreement from the founder and offering franchises without ever having operated a single location for a single day. Successful franchise systems are built from the ground up, with the original founder getting his or her hands dirty and toiling long, hard hours to make their system a success. Steer clear of "concept sellers" who have no experience in making each unit work.

The exploration of the franchisor's history is one of the most important tasks you will undertake during your search for and purchase of the right franchise for you. The focus of your investigation is Items 1, 2, 3, and 4 of the UFOC along with the financial statements. The Appendix contains examples of how these sections actually look. In exploring this history, or lack of it, there are some telltale signs to look for and, in some cases, guard against.

One of the first signs is the general appearance of the disclosure document itself. Is it put together in a professional manner and presented to you as the law requires? (Comparison of the disclosure document under review to the UFOC in the Appendix is a good place to start). Did the franchisor operate this business as an independent business before franchising or has it been in existence only a short while, using other people's capital to develop the concept? A short history may indicate this. A quick review of "The Loser's Circle's" offering circular revealed the answer to all of these questions.

Another telltale sign to look for is a list of numerous predecessor companies or spin-off corporations which may have been created only to confuse your investigation of the principals behind the franchise. Not all franchise companies with complex structures (having multiple levels of corporations and subsidiaries) are out to take advantage of franchise purchasers. Many have legitimate reasons for complex corporate structures. Just make sure you understand the reasons for multiple companies and subsidiaries if you find them. For an example of this see Item 1 of the UFOC found in the Appendix.

UFOC Item 1 sets forth the company history. The guidelines require a complete history, including an identification of any predecessors and affiliates. The history must explain when franchises were first offered. This item also covers application of any special laws or regulations affecting the operation of the franchise business.

The true history, however, may best be revealed in the people behind the organization. Closely study Item 2 of the UFOC which discusses the background and history of the individuals who operate the franchise company. This history is limited to 5 years but generally offers good insight into the employment background of all officers, directors and sales personnel. Note the length of time the key officials have been with the system. Also, determine what connection the key people have to the origins of the company. As we saw in "The Loser's Circle" situation, a weak connection to the operation of the units in the system can be a telltale sign that demands closer inspection. While some will argue that in most instances it is desirable to have the vision of the founders still involved in the company, there are many instances where a business built by one type of person (entrepreneur) is better operated by another type of person (manager).

But in either case, good franchisors understand how important the connection between the operation of the individual units, restaurants or stores is to the operation of a good franchise system. Many companies insist that their executives spend time working in franchised units and stores to keep in touch with the lifeblood of the system—find out if this is a policy in the systems you are considering.

Items 3 and 4 deal with the "dark side" of the company and its officers' histories. Litigation and bankruptcies over the last 10 years are the focus of these items. Look to see if the company or any of its key officials have been involved with or connected to any bankruptcies, franchise or securities litigation, or had any fraud actions brought against them. The company is only as strong and vital as the people who run it.

If any bankruptcies or litigation matters are reported, investigate them further. Use the information provided to contact the court where the action was filed and confirm the reported information. If a litigation action involves an existing or former franchisee, try to contact them and determine what gave rise to the dispute. Again, not all reported litigation is a harbinger of ill tidings about the franchisor. Franchisees can be just as much a source of problems that give rise to legal actions as franchisors. But all reported litigation and bankruptcy episodes should be closely studied and investigated.

One of the officers of the "The Loser Circle" franchise disclosed a prior bankruptcy history. This was a warning that no one heeded. Don't invest much faith in the old tale that "so and so went broke 10 times before becoming a millionaire"—1 out of 10 is not very good odds.

With the exception of the very large franchising companies, it is always advisable to meet the officers of the company face-to-face to determine if the description you find in the disclosure documents fits the personality and character of the persons you meet. This "first impression" can be very important. Trust your instincts. If there is something that troubles you about this encounter, follow through to determine if your instincts are correct. Make sure you like the business and professional personality of the organization and its main people.

Because the personal histories contained in the disclosure documents may tend to be more of a sales tool than a realistic history of the individuals, other sources of information on these individuals may be helpful. This is another area where professional assistance can help you in your research.

Another important item in exploring the history of the franchisor is its financial background. Financial information can be obtained from many different sources these days. If the franchisor is a listed company, annual reports and SEC findings are available from any stockbroker. Dun and Bradstreet carries credit ratings and other vital information on unlisted companies. A visit to your local library or other information source may disclose some important financial information. If you are computer-literate the Internet offers a wealth of business and financial information. To dig a little deeper you may ask your accountant to do some further investigative work.

You might want to get a credit report from an agency like TRW or Trans Union. These companies provide reports of varied scope. It may cost several hundred dollars to obtain an independent litigation and regulatory search, but if you are about to make the largest business investment in your life, it may be well worth the money for independent verification regarding the credit and character of a franchisor. The financial stability of the franchisor is very important because it is the keystone holding up the franchise arch (no pun intended). If the franchisor fails, your franchise could tumble down with it and your unit would be worthless.

Some of the state and federal agencies which oversee the franchising industry can be of great assistance in helping you investigate the history of the franchisor. State Attorney General's offices or the FTC will normally know of complaints and actions taken against franchisors which may not be listed in disclosure documents. Discovery of this crucial information can be a key factor in making your final decision. With a little persistence you can flush out franchisors who have persistent problems with government agencies or their franchisees.

Another barometer of how a system operates—and the pride its officials take in the system—can be found in company-operated units. Not all franchisors operate direct units, some leave this exclusively to franchisees. But most systems do maintain company-operated locations. Ask to see the direct operation units. These should be run as "showcase" units—ready to show off the best the system has to offer. Ask to be taken behind the scenes. Find out how the franchisor hires and trains managers for these locations and whether the same techniques are shared with franchisees.

If the company-operated locations do not meet your expectations or lack the "showcase" quality you demand, then you should think about whether this is the right system for you. These units are a direct reflection of the company's pride in its product or service.

10

INVESTIGATING EXISTING FRANCHISEES

While the disclosure documents and information will help you determine the history of the franchisor and the particulars of the franchise offering, investigating the franchisor's relationship with existing franchisees will result in the best hands-on information you can get.

To begin your investigation, simply check the list which should be attached to your disclosure documents. If there is no list—and the franchisor has franchisees—the franchisor is in violation of the law and you should be highly suspicious. And, you should begin to wonder what the franchisor has to hide. See Item 20 of the UFOC in the Appendix to see how this disclosure is made; most of the historical information is displayed in chart form.

The number of franchisees appearing on the list depends on the disclosure format used by the franchisor. Under the UFOC format, a franchisor is required to list the 100 geographically-closest franchisees (if that many or more exist), while only the 10 geographically-closest franchisees must be disclosed under the FTC format. In practice most franchisors, except for the long established franchise systems, list all of their franchisees. If there are no franchisees that fact should be clearly stated.

First, review the list. Get a feel for the franchisor's system. Where are franchises located, and which, if any, are similar in terms of population, size and exposure to the site you may have in mind.

The list should include the names, addresses, and telephone numbers of each franchisee. This information is provided for one reason only: so that you may contact them. Take advantage of this list. Spend as many days as you need to contact each and every franchisee on the list. This will not only give you realistic information about the franchisor but will be the first *independent* information about the actual operation of your franchise and the primary source of information on the kind of relationship you can expect to have with the franchisor. If any of the franchisees are having a particularly difficult time with a franchisor you can bet they will be more than happy to share it with you. Listen carefully to what they have to say.

Had "The Loser's Circle's" buyers taken the time to speak to the franchisees listed, they may have uncovered the fraud that awaited them. Especially in that experience, asking the right questions, and investigating the "first" franchisee's background and relationship, would have unearthed a wealth of important information.

Contacting franchisees may lead to invitations to visit their locations. You should visit as many as possible. This will provide keen insight into your new business. The franchisees will acquaint you with the advantages and disadvantages of the franchisor's system and how much influence franchisees have with the franchisor. This is also your best opportunity to check on what comparable franchise units are earning in terms of revenue. People are more likely to be frank and open in a personal meeting, particularly if they know you are considering becoming their future business associate. This unhurried, face-to-face contact usually permits you to ask and them to answer some of the questions that are more difficult over the phone.

If there are regional franchisee associations, visit the leader of the one in your part of the country. Find out why it was formed, what purposes it serves and what benefits and burdens will apply if you join (a typical example is a regional TV advertising campaign which you will be obligated to help pay for).

The franchisor may suggest specific franchisees for you to contact but it is not advisable to contact only these franchisees. Again, do your own investigation and get in touch with as many franchisees as you can and learn what you can from this first hand, independent information.

Some of the questions you should ask are:

- How long did it take them to break-even?
- How much money did they originally invest?
- What are their annual revenues?
- How much profit are they making based upon actual sales, etc.?
- What ongoing assistance has the franchisor provided?
- How is the quality of the services or products provided by the franchisor?
- Has the franchisor regularly conducted meetings with franchisees?
- Is the franchisee aware of other franchisees who are not satisfied with or who have had problems with the franchisor?
- What, if any, terms of the franchise agreement may be negotiable?
- Does the franchisor appear to be concerned with the long range development of the system?
- Is the advertising required by the franchisor effective?
- What assistance was available during the grand opening phase?

- Does the franchisor conduct periodic inspections of the locations in the franchise system?
- Has the franchisor directed advertising funds from the national fund to the franchisee's marketing area?
- Does the franchise system offer any form of buying cooperatives?
- How has the franchisor treated franchisees upon renewal?
- Has the operations manual met their expectations?
- How was the training program?
- What type of communication is provided for between the franchisor and franchisees, and is it effective?
- How has the franchise resolved disputes?

As you can see there are a multitude of questions you can ask. The experiences of existing franchisees are invaluable. *Nothing else will provide you with a more realistic view of the franchise operation that you are investigating.*

Existing franchisees are a unique source of information on the financial data important to your decision. Where else can you poll existing locations on the possible results of your future business? As will be discussed in greater detail in the next chapter, franchise companies are reluctant to provide meaningful earnings information. Part of the reason for this is that prohibitive regulations exist curtailing the presentation of financial earnings information to potential buyers. While the regulations are intended to prevent fraudulent or negligently prepared earnings statements, they also deter solid franchise companies from presenting any financial estimates about prospective franchises. These regulations, however, do not bar existing franchisees from providing profit and loss results to potential franchise investors. As a result, existing franchisees may be your only source of this most important aspect of your purchasing decision. Even when financial information is provided by a franchise company, existing franchisees can confirm or deny the information provided by the company.

Remember that the "family of franchisees" is one of the benefits you gain when buying a franchise. Drawing upon this resource in the purchasing phase allows you to secure information which may not be otherwise available. Take advantage of the opportunity. Some of the most valuable information is right there for the taking.

As part of your criteria in selecting a franchise, add the existence of a franchise council to your list. If one is not in place, find out if the franchisor has any serious plans to establish one. If one is established, how is it composed, who are the present members, how are franchisees elected or appointed, and does it have effective input? When you become a franchisee, work to make the franchisee council a meaningful part of the system. Good franchise systems do not establish adversarial relationships with their franchisees, they seek to make franchisees an indispensable part of the system.

After speaking with the franchisees, revisit your cash flow projections and review the assumptions underlying each scenario. Compare these with the information supplied by the franchisees and make any necessary modifications.

11

EARNINGS CLAIMS

Earn $100,000 your first year! $50,000 profit guaranteed! You can't lose! If you don't earn $100,000 we will buy it back!

This was the kind of promise that drew in the vending machine buyers we met in the first chapter. The no-risk-big-money proposition is hard for some people to resist. They innately trust people and believe they will stand by their word. This is why "earnings claims" and "guaranteed buy-back" offers are so dangerous—and highly regulated.

These claims are designed to attract your attention...and they are effective. Let's face it, everyone wants to become wealthy. Unfortunately, unethical business opportunity sellers and franchisors know this so, beware. When dollar signs begin to flash in your eyes you can get hooked by what a salesperson is trying to sell. Do not be a victim of your understandable but dangerous desire to get rich quick. Buying a franchise is a big step and a salesperson's claims are simply not enough. You must get the facts.

Making earnings claims, like those above, may be illegal, and are rarely made by reputable franchisors. The FTC Rule and many state laws prohibit franchisors from making earnings claims *unless* adequate documentation of the specific claim is provided to you as part of the disclosure documents.

Regulators are confronted with a dilemma when faced with the issue of earning claims: how to provide potential franchisees with important information without misleading them in the process.

One problem with developing a uniform rule that requires all franchisors to disclose earning estimates to potential buyers, is that franchising cuts across many different industries, each, to some degree, using different financial measurements. Another is how to handle new franchise systems that have no history or solid financial experience that can be used as a basis for fair estimates or representations of potential earnings.

Because of this dilemma, regulators have settled on the system devised in the early days of franchising: *franchisors are not required to make any disclosure of expected earnings and, unless they provide financial estimates in accordance with certain guidelines, are legally prohibited from doing so.*

Recent revisions to the UFOC Guidelines liberalized some of the rules about the disclosure of earnings claims but did not address franchisors' hesitancy completely. As a result, some franchise companies provide earnings information to franchise buyers while others do not.

Under the UFOC Guidelines, the basic rules governing earnings claims are that:

- they must be included in the Offering Circular (Item 19)
- they must have a reasonable basis at the time they are made
- they must include a detailed description of their factual basis and the material assumptions underlying their preparation and presentation
- the franchisor must present or offer to present (upon the buyer's request) substantiating information to support the claims

The Item 19 Guidelines do not require franchisors to format financial claims in a certain way, or to use any specific methodology such as averages, gross profit, net profit, gross sales or the like.

While this liberalized approach encourages more franchise companies to present earnings claims, it does not necessarily allow franchise buyers to compare "apples to apples". Different companies in the same business category may present financial earnings information in different formats and methodologies. If you're buying a franchise, you must try to understand each franchisor's claims and then, if possible, compare them to other offerings.

The bottom line is this: *if any type of earnings or financial claim is made, the franchisor must provide you with specific information regarding the claim in the Offering Circular. If an earnings or financial claim is made outside of the Offering Circular, either verbally or in writing, you should be suspicious.* The proverbial "cocktail napkin" disclosure is strictly prohibited. Likewise, if a claim is made but the franchise company is unable to produce substantiating information, then it may be time to look elsewhere or to probe the franchisor further until you have this important information.

Because of misconceptions about what an earnings claim really is, even well-intentioned, honest franchisors innocently violate the rules. For instance, it is common to come across franchise executives who believe it is okay to disclose actual sales figures from company-operated or franchise locations—because "it is the truth, the real numbers, what's wrong with that?" The fact of the matter is that the "real numbers" are subject to the same regulations as average or projected numbers. All earnings claims must be presented with the same opportunity to review the underlying source information and must have a reasonable basis from which they are taken. The fact that they may be "real numbers" is only the first step in making a proper earnings claim disclosure.

You should carefully analyze any information presented to substantiate earnings claims. Earnings of company-run retail units, for example, are often presented as a basis for earnings claims. This seems reasonable at face value, *but company-run operations may benefit from amenities or payment of expenses which are recorded in different ways.* Certain hidden "economies of scale" may skew the bottom line numbers. Some state franchise examiners require special disclaimers be placed on earnings claims derived from company-run operations. If the earnings claim is based upon a company-run operation, you and your accountant should ask incisive questions to determine how the figures were derived and what relationship they bear to your future operation.

If you are proposing to buy an existing operation, run either by a departing franchisee or the company itself, Item 19 is flexible enough to permit franchisors to share the actual financial information regarding that particular location with you. When you are considering this type of purchase, obtaining the actual financial history of the operation is a must. Nothing else will give you a better opportunity to predict future success.

In summary, dealing with franchisors who offer earnings information is better than dealing with those who do not. However, dealing with earnings claims is tricky business. Make sure the claims are presented in accordance with the law and that you verify the source of the information. Investigating the company's claims by discussing them with established franchisees will match the estimates and projections to reality. Do not be deceived, by yourself or a franchisor, into believing that a franchisor's claim is a guarantee of what you can expect.

Unfortunately, the realization of poor earnings may come only after you have invested your hard earned dollars and sweat equity. This can be one of the biggest disappointments you will encounter once your franchise is operating. To avoid this unhappy event, make certain the franchisor provides substantiation and that, if the documentation is provided, you review it with great care.

III

NEGOTIATING FOR AND BUYING A FRANCHISE

12

UNDERSTANDING AND NEGOTIATING THE FRANCHISE AGREEMENT

Once you've made the important decision to purchase the franchise unit, the next hurdle is the contract. Your legal relationship with the franchisor begins and ends with the franchise agreement and everything we've discussed to this point leads to signing this agreement. *At this crucial juncture you must do your best to see your systematic plan through to the end.* First, take time to understand the agreement. Second, prepare yourself to negotiate the agreement to your best advantage (the first is easier to accomplish than the second). To gain a basic understanding of what you might expect, turn to the Franchise Agreement in the Appendix.

It was noted in a Congressional Committee Report, after extensive hearings on franchising before the Committee on Small Business, that:

> Current regulatory efforts seek to remedy the serious "imbalance" of information between franchisors and potential franchisees in solicitations and sales of franchises. An equally serious imbalance of power exists between these parties *after the franchise agreement is initiated* and throughout the ongoing relationship. Advantages of financial strength, access to information and to legal advice *create a gross disparity of bargaining power in favor of the franchisor* that results

in one-sided franchise agreements that are offered, and generally accepted, on a take-it-or-leave-it basis. (Emphasis added)

As you can see from this report, the first thing to accept, before you even begin to review your contract, is that you are at a distinct disadvantage. The reason is simple. *The franchisor and its legal advisors have prepared and invested a great deal of time and money in structuring the contract for their own protection.* In addition, since a franchise company needs uniformity, efficiency and control, franchise agreements have become as standardized as insurance contracts. This is why your chances of understanding the franchise agreement are much better than your chances of changing it. Franchisors resist changing an individual franchisee's contract with a vengeance, which is not to say that all franchise agreements are unfair or non-negotiable. But again: most will be heavily weighted in favor of the franchise company and you can expect staunch resistance to change.

Working to remove the imbalance is called "negotiation". Unfortunately, as noted in the Congressional Report, many franchisors do view their contracts as a "take-it-or-leave-it" proposition. Either you accept their terms or they will look for another franchisee. From the franchisor's perspective, there is good reason for this inflexibility: the desire to maintain uniformity throughout the franchisor's system. Franchise companies like to keep the duties imposed on them, as well as the franchisees, nearly identical in every franchise agreement. Practically speaking this makes sense for the franchisor, but not all franchisees or franchise locations are identical. Further, some franchise companies carry the mantle of uniformity to extreme ends when, in reality, they seek only to maintain the legal advantage.

Before you seek to change it, gain a solid understanding of the contents of the franchise agreement. Unlike the new "plain English" requirement in place for Offering Circulars, "legalese" is the standard fare of franchise agreements. Nevertheless, reading about and understanding the legal relationship which you are about to enter, will serve you well as you proceed in your discussions with the franchise company.

It is hard to recall how many times clients have come through my door with a franchise problem *after they signed the contract* and start off by revealing that they never read the contract itself. Many say they just didn't want to take the time, while others embarrassedly admit that they relied on what the sales representative told them. When it is pointed out that the "problem" that brought them into the office is clearly spelled out in the franchise agreement—*in the franchisor's favor*—their only recourse is to plead brain death.

Most franchise agreements are lengthy documents covering every conceivable aspect of your relationship. Actually, a good place to start your review is at the very end of the agreement. Here you will find a lot of legal "boilerplate" that will control the balance of the document. Although we will separately discuss some of the boilerplate topics in detail later in this chapter, these provisions usually receive the least attention from franchise buyers but generally have the greatest impact on the outcome of disputes with the franchisor. These clauses normally control how, when and where disputes with your franchisor will be resolved. They deserve your considerable attention and understanding. For a sampling of these important clauses see Sections 12, 15 and 17 of the Franchise Agreement in the Appendix.

A typical franchise contract divides the duties imposed on the franchisee and the franchisor into separate sections. Many of the franchisee's duties are ongoing. You are generally required to:

- make all payments on time
- contribute to an advertising fund and/or expend a certain amount on local advertising

- use the system's trademarks and service marks in a pre-determined manner
- abide by the operations manual in conducting the business
- conduct business within a defined territory or at a specific location
- attend the mandatory training program
- maintain certain business hours, and so forth

See Section 7 of the Franchise Agreement in the Appendix for the typical obligations placed on franchisees.

The franchisor's duties are mostly immediate and not ongoing. They are usually required to:

- grant a specific territory
- provide training
- issue an operations manual
- help with the grand opening
- assist with the purchase of equipment and inventory
- administer the advertising requirements
- approve the initial location
- offer initial assistance and advice for a set period of time
- buy from designated suppliers

See Section 8 of the Franchise Agreement in the Appendix for the typical obligations placed on franchisors.

A close review of the franchise agreement will reveal that the duties imposed on the franchisor diminish after the start-up phase of the relationship. Ongoing assistance is usually couched in discretionary terms. That is, beyond the initial start-up duties, the only requirements placed on the franchisor are very loosely stated or non-existent.

The key to a good contractual relationship is clarity. All parties have a vested interest in making sure that their legal blueprint is readable and understandable. You will encounter language that you do not understand or which could be better crafted to define the duties that are included. Franchisors are generally not overly resistant to clarifying the language of the franchise agreement. So let this be your negotiating starting point: seek to clarify confusing language. *And once the franchisor has agreed to make clarification changes, a negotiating climate is established, and more substantive changes can be requested with a better chance of success.*

Make sure you understand each provision of your franchise agreement. Review it with your legal advisor. This can go a long way in avoiding future surprises and disappointment. And, starting with items that require only clarification will set a fair tone for more important negotiations.

A solid understanding of your and the franchisor's duties under the contract is your launching pad for successful negotiations. Since you will have only limited success in obtaining negotiated changes, it is important to study the agreement to find those items which are of true importance. When you identify your "deal killer" provisions you will be ready to approach the franchisor with your negotiation strategy.

Some of the items which will prove difficult to change, but which you should consider negotiating, are:

- the length of the agreement
- the purchase price for your franchise
- financing terms
- size of territory
- exclusivity of territory
- renewal terms
- assignability (or sale), and possibly equipment purchase requirements

From a legal viewpoint some of the areas of concern which should be discussed are:

- choice of the law governing the contract
- selected forum for disputes
- arbitration of disputes

See Section 15 of the Franchise Agreement in the Appendix for an example of the first two types of clauses.

These are just a few of the areas warranting your attention and effort. One word of caution here. Ironically, if the franchisor appears too willing to change the contract terms, you should wonder how much uniformity the franchisor's system has. Remember, the franchisor uses the contract to achieve some semblance of uniformity throughout the system. If the franchisor is willing to make unfettered accommodations for you, there is some question as to what type of changes have been made for others. This is an important area to discuss with existing franchisees. Nothing prevents you or existing franchisees from sharing the terms of existing contracts. This does not guarantee, of course, that your terms will be the same or that the franchisor will be willing to accommodate every franchisee in the same way. It does, however, give you some direction in your negotiations.

When negotiating with the franchisor do not overlook the assistance you can obtain from your attorney. The involvement of your attorney alone may place you on a more equal footing with the franchisor. Your attorney can assist in:

- reviewing the Offering Circular and franchise agreement
- determining points for clarification and negotiation
- preparing for the negotiations

- making appropriate proposals
- operating as a sounding board for your proposals

Once at the negotiating table, your attorney can help articulate some of your ideas and proposals, and ultimately make certain that they are properly drafted and included in the franchise agreement.

Although you should rely on your attorney for a certain amount of assistance, there is no substitute for your own careful reading and review of the contract. Again, this contract will be the basis of your relationship with the franchisor and you can not always count on the person you have dealt with remaining with the company or being willing to make good on a promise consummated by a handshake rather than the written word.

Thoroughly reading the contract will also provide you with a good understanding of what is required of you and the franchisor and you should make a list of what is required of you both. This will enable you to better understand the contract and help you decide whether you feel uncomfortable with some of the conditions of the contract.

Now compare the franchise agreement to the Offering Circular. *Everything that is promised or stated in the Circular should appear in the franchise agreement in one form or another.* This comparison is now easier under the new UFOC format because specific reference to the pertinent sections of the contract is required in the matching disclosure item of the Offering Circular. If a discrepancy exists, this matter should be straightened out before a contract is signed. As an exercise, compare the UFOC to the Franchise Agreement in the Appendix for discrepancies.

We now turn to the details of some of the specific areas for negotiation.

PURCHASE PRICE NEGOTIATIONS

An important item to think about negotiating is the price. How much will you have to pay? Also, once the amount is established, how will you be required to pay? Although this may be one of the more difficult areas in which to succeed, there are many variants in the sale of a franchise, and you may be lucky enough to find something that gives you a negotiating edge on the purchase price. For example, perhaps your franchise is in new and untried territory that the franchisor is eager to expand into. Or maybe it's in a city where rents and other costs are higher.

Your negotiations in this area should not be limited to the initial franchise fee, the one charged at the beginning of the relationship. There are a number of other "fees" imposed on a franchisee during the franchise relationship: royalty payments, advertising fees, renewal fees, and, in some systems, product purchase or service fees requirements. *In your review of the Offering Circular and franchise agreement, you should highlight each fee and determine how each will affect your bottom line.* As noted before, most of the fees are set forth in Items 5, 6 and 7 of the Offering Circular. However, the franchise agreement is the place to verify these amounts and to determine if any other fees exist. See Sections 2 and 3 in the Franchise Agreement in the Appendix. Once you are clear on the fees to be charged, you should assess whether any reason or leverage ("edge") exists to gain a reduction.

If you ask for a price reduction and the franchisor turns you down, don't hesitate to use the refusal as the basis for asking for something else; a longer-term agreement, for example, or a larger territory. *Your negotiating point is: if you have to pay a higher price than it's worth, the franchisor should give you more time to amortize your investment or more territory from which to draw profits.*

Purchase price negotiations must be evaluated on a case by case basis. Some franchisors are very inflexible in this area. Others, however, are willing to negotiate price as well as terms of payment. Many times the degree of flexibility is a function of how eager the franchisor is to sell the franchise. If you are the first franchisee in the system or the only individual interested in a given area, then the sheer lack of competition may give you the upper hand in price negotiations. If, however, there are other potential purchasers or the planned territory is easy to sell, your leverage may not be as great.

You may have greater success seeking financing or payment plan options from the franchisor. The UFOC Guidelines require franchisors to disclose in Item 10 any financing arrangements they offer or arrange. See Item 10 in the UFOC in the Appendix for the standard language when financing is not available. Obviously this is the first place to look. But, don't stop there. Although disclosure of financing arrangements is required, it is not illegal on your end to ask or obtain a financing arrangement which has not been specifically disclosed. In addition, while the franchisor may not have intended to offer financing when the Offering Circular was prepared, the reality of making sales sometimes softens the franchisor's initial policies. The best areas to seek financing options are the initial franchise fee and equipment and inventory purchases. Be prepared for strong resistance, however. Just like anyone else, franchisors want as much money up front as they can get.

The lesson here is not to overlook the possibility of negotiating fees with the franchisor. Of course the more popular the franchise, the higher the fees and the stronger the resistance to negotiation. But fees, in the right circumstances, can be negotiated. *And if you can't get a lower price, you might get something else to make up for it.* Look for the right opportunity and be prepared to give it a try. What do you have to lose? The worst that can happen is that you end up paying the franchisor's asking price. *Don't be afraid to negotiate price.*

INITIAL TERM
AND RENEWAL CLAUSES

The next item which is sometimes up for negotiation is the length of the contract. When you purchase a franchise, unbelievable as it may seem, you are not purchasing it forever. Most franchise agreements are structured in five or ten year intervals with renewal options thereafter. See Sections 1 and 8 of the Franchise Agreement in the Appendix. Remember, what you are purchasing is the right to operate your business as a unit of the franchise. If the franchisor terminates that right, then you are out of business as a franchise unit since you have no "equity" in the franchise business. The term and renewal clauses are crucial to your ablity to sell the business as an operating unit of the franchise. After all, if the franchisor can terminate your right to operate the business after a short period of time, you have nothing to sell. Let us expand on this important point:

A business that currently provides ongoing income or an income stream, can only be sold if that income will continue (if it can be projected to roll over in enough years to justify the investment). If the term is too short to "amortize" the required investment, or if the term is ending *without free right to renew*, then the business can't be sold and is virtually worthless.

Also, because money has a "time value" (it's worth more to receive money sooner than later because it can be invested) the price for a business is generally calculated by arriving at the "present value" of the projected income stream. For example, if a business brings in profit of $50,000 per year after all expenses, it can be expected to bring in $500,000 over 10 years, the usual term of a franchise agreement (expanded profits due to inflation are exluded). With a full ten year term, that business is worth the present value of that $500,000 income stream. *That very same* *business with only 2 years left under the franchise agreement and no renewal rights will only be worth the present value of the $100,000 income stream ($50,000 a year for 2 years), if it can be sold at all.* Even though franchisee-advocates complain that franchisees are entitled to some recognition for the "equity" or "goodwill" of the franchise business, and some states restrict uncompensated terminations, *the franchise relationship is purely contractual and most franchise agreements do not call for any payment to a franchisee upon termination.* Because of this, the contractual provisions controlling the length of the relationship and the ability to continue or renew the relationship deserve some attention and, if possible, negotiation.

Generally speaking, the longer the term of the agreement the better. If you are purchasing a really "hot" franchise, you'll want to protect your right to operate the business for as long as possible. Or, if the franchise requires a large capital expenditure (a restaurant, motel or hotel) which can only be recouped over a definitive period of time, you need to make sure that the initial term of the agreement is long enough so your capital is returned and you earn a profit. Other considerations, when analyzing the length of the franchise agreement, include: the length of a real estate lease; the term of any financing; the life-cycle of any required equipment or computers, and your own assessment of the longevity of the franchise concept.

At a minimum, your franchise agreement should specify the initial contract term and address renewal options. For instance, the initial grant of the franchise may be for five years, with the right to renew for an additional five year period. Try to get an indefinite number of renewals rather than a limited number. As will be discussed below, franchisors generally set forth renewal criteria which must be met at the end of each term before allowing the relationship to continue. Your position on obtaining an unlimited number of renewals should simply be that *if you can meet the criteria at the time of each renewal why should there be any limitation on the number of times you can renew?*

As mentioned, franchise agreements usually contain renewal conditions or criteria. See Section 8 of the Franchise Agreement in the Appendix. These conditions should be precisely understood at the beginning of the relationship. Some of the conditions include:

- the payment of a renewal fee
- the execution of a new franchise agreement (usually the agreement offered to new franchisees)
- a requirement to update your format and business equipment, or to establish new outlets in your geographical territory

Some of the conditions may relate to your past performance, such as achieving a certain level of sales, the number of times you defaulted on your obligations during the last term or the regularity of your payments to the franchisor. Make sure that each standard or condition is objectively stated, easily analyzed and clearly written. It could be the difference between business failure and a healthy continuing relationship.

Franchisees often fail to realize the implications of the requirement to enter into a new franchise agreement at the beginning of each renewal term. That is, the original agreement you painstakingly negotiated may be thrown out the window only to be replaced by a less advantageous agreement. Franchisors justify this requirement by reverting to the "need for uniformity" argument. They contend that—as the system matures and the terms of the standard franchise agreement are revised—at some point most or all franchisees should be signed up on the same agreement. The justification often continues with "and we don't want to discriminate between our franchisees—so we must insist that at the time of renewal all of our franchisees enter into the franchise agreement then offered to new franchisees".

When analyzed closely, this justification is really quite thin. *It ignores the fact that long-time franchisees took a greater risk by investing when the franchise was younger and shakier.* A study of the evolution of a franchise agreement in any franchise system would likely reveal that the only revisions made *benefit the franchise company*—usually an increase in certain fees or a strengthening of general contractual provisions—not the franchisees. As franchise systems grow in popularity there is a tendency to increase the fees for royalties, advertising and initial start up—the demand allows the franchisor to simply ask for more and get it. While few would argue against franchisors being allowed to raise fees for new franchisees, passing these increases on to existing loyal franchisees at renewal time can be unfair and overreaching.

To prevent increases at renewal time you must stand firm during the initial negotiations. You may have better leverage if you are one of the early franchisees in a new system, before the die is cast. In any event, working to keep the terms of the franchise agreement the same as the day you entered into the agreement may be difficult but is a most worthwhile effort.

Again, *the time to negotiate the renewal conditions is when the contract is signed not when the renewal option comes in to play.* More specifically, some of the areas you would hope to have negotiated and resolved in your favor are: the payment of a renewal fee; conditions of updating; and, as noted above, freezing the terms of your existing franchise contract. It is at renewal time that the franchisor takes the opportunity, especially if the system is growing rapidly, to increase the royalty payments which you will be required to pay. If you agree at the outset to sign a new franchise agreement upon each renewal, you are opening yourself up to royalty increases at each renewal.

FRANCHISE TERMINATION

Termination goes hand-in-hand with renewal. *Thoroughly review your contract for the conditions of termination,* both how you may terminate the relationship and how the franchisor may terminate your franchise. Section 9 of the Franchise Agreement in the Appendix will give you some insight into how these clauses may appear. When it comes to termination by the franchisee, most franchise agreements are silent, generally only the franchisor's ability to terminate is discussed. However, circumstances may arise when the franchisee wants to terminate the relationship. Since the franchise relationship depends on certain duties being performed by the franchisor, if the franchisor fails to perform those duties, the franchisee may want to end the relationship. Therefore, you may wish to negotiate some termination conditions which would allow you to escape from the agreement and recover some of your money *if the franchisor breaches the agreement and your business or financial condition suffers because of it.*

Carefully review each ground for termination by the franchisor. These are generally labeled as "defaults", or breaches of the agreement by the franchisee. Make sure each ground is clear, objective and easily understood. Typically, a franchisor may terminate a franchise agreement if the franchisee:

- makes an assignment for the benefit of creditors
- files a voluntary petition in bankruptcy or is adjudicated as bankrupt or insolvent
- fails to continuously and actively operate the business
- fails to pay when due royalty fees or other fees
- fails to submit when due periodic or annual financial statements or other information
- operates the business in a manner that presents a health or safety hazard

- makes an unauthorized assignment of the franchise agreement or the franchise
- has made any material misrepresentations or misstatements on his or her application
- fails to meet minimum operation standards set forth in the franchise agreement
- commits multiple defaults of the franchise agreement, whether or not cured

Pay particular attention to whether the franchisor is required to give you "notice" of specific defaults and whether any "cure periods or grace periods" are provided. Since not everyone meets all of their technical obligations all of the time, build in sufficient time to correct any defaults that may arise. This can be accomplished by eliminating automatic termination clauses, requiring written notice of defaults and seeking adequate cure periods of 10 days or more, particularly in situations where the franchisee may not know whether his or her actions may be deemed a default in the mind of the franchisor. *While franchisors are normally unwilling to change the default clause of an agreement, they may be more susceptible to persuasion with respect to "technical" defaults (as opposed to "payment defaults").*

Some franchise companies divide defaults into categories of severity. They may insist upon automatic termination with no opportunity to cure for the most serious and obvious defaults, such as failure to pay royalty fees, but provide notice and cure periods for less severe, less obvious defaults, such as failing to follow system standards. Take the time to consider whether a "no cure" default is fair and workable in a given circumstance and whether the length of any cure periods provided are sufficient to permit a good faith correction.

Spending time to familiarize yourself with the termination or default section of your franchise agreement is time well spent.

Although some states, as noted before, do have protective relationship laws restricting the unfettered termination of a franchise, there is no substitute for personal vigilance and the negotiation of favorable contractual terms at the outset of the franchise relationship.

TRANSFERRING OR SELLING THE FRANCHISE

Under most franchise agreements, you will be given certain conditional rights to sell your franchise to a third party. Section 11 of the Franchise Agreement in the Appendix is a good example of what you might expect to see. If this right does not appear, you should negotiate for one. Nothing could be worse than investing all your time and money in developing a business only to learn that you are unrealistically restricted when it comes time to sell it. Your business, if it is properly run, is a growing asset. You hope to make money from operating it, *but when it comes time to sell the business or leave it to your children, you will want to realize all of the value that you worked so hard to build.*

Carefully review the conditions upon which you may ultimately sell your franchise. Many franchise agreements contain a "first right of refusal" by the franchisor. This means that if you receive a *bona fide* (real) offer to sell the franchise, the franchisor then has the first right to purchase the franchise from you at the *bona fide* price. Some contend that the franchisor's right of first refusal is an impediment to a smooth sale since it causes a delay and places the potential buyer in the position of "price guinea pig", allowing the franchisor to "shop" the sale price. In practice, however, most franchisors, if asked to cooperate in advance, will inform the selling franchisee *whether the franchisor has any interest in buying the franchise business. In most cases the franchisor will opt to allow the sale to a third party to proceed. After all, the franchisor's main business goal is generally to sell franchise units, not to buy them.*

Most franchise agreements also contain the franchisor's "right of approval" of a new franchisee. Just as the franchisor accepted you into the system based upon certain criteria, the same conditions will apply to a new franchisee. It is important, however, that the franchisor not unreasonably withhold this right of approval. Make certain that your franchise agreement contains a statement that the franchisor may not unreasonably withhold its consent. *Generally the franchisor has every reason to want the sale to go through, provided that:*

- *the purchaser will be an effective franchisee (that his or her character, business experience and credit rating are satisfactory to the franchisor) and is willing to comply with the franchise agreement in all respects and satisfactorily complete the training program*
- *the selling franchisee pays any and all debts owed to the franchisor*

If the agreement form does not so specify, ask for a provision stating that the franchisor will not withhold consent, provided that these conditions are met.

Another concern in this area is the ease with which your business may be passed along to your family. Many people develop a business so that it may be passed on to their sons and daughters. Others, as part of a comprehensive estate plan, want protective clauses in the agreement in case of unplanned events such as death or disability. If you have this in mind, terms addressing this should appear in the final franchise agreement. Most franchise agreements provide for this contingency but the conditions of this "right of survivorship" must be closely scrutinized—check to make sure that the conditions are not so stringent as to be impossible to perform. See Section 10 of the Franchise Agreement in the Appendix.

The franchisor has the same interest in an orderly transfer upon inheritance as it does regarding a sale and should be willing to agree not to withhold its consent, provided its concerns are met (satisfactory character, experience and credit of the successor and payment of any debts to the franchisor), in the same manner as a sale. And fairness requires one more provision regarding the death of the franchisee: permission for the interim operation of the franchise unit by an executor or administrator, until the successor party is able to take over.

PRODUCT AND EQUIPMENT PURCHASE REQUIREMENTS

Another area of consideration is the equipment and product requirements set forth in the franchise agreement. Many franchise systems are based on the reproduction or sale of unique products. On some occasions, the franchisor is also the manufacturer or distributor of the franchised product or the equipment necessary to reproduce the product. In other systems, products and equipment may be acquired from outside vendors, some of whom may have a special affiliation or contractual arrangement with the franchisor.

Franchisors have a legitimate interest in maintaining product uniformity and quality. Uniform products and formats are the essence of franchising. Franchisors often control uniformity and quality by controlling the source of the product or its ingredients. Sometimes, special equipment is necessary to reproduce the product.

Understanding the products and equipment required under the franchise agreement should be a major focus of your *contract review*. The UFOC and the franchise agreement should set this out clearly. Determine the cost of the required equipment and whether any restrictions apply on where it can be purchased. Further:

- can the products or equipment be obtained from sources other than the franchisor or a specified vendor and,
- if not, is the current pricing structure competitive?
- what protection is there to guard against unfair price increases in the future?
- are discounts available for buying within the system's purchasing channels?
- is there a "substitute approval" provision in the agreement, allowing franchisees to seek approval to make purchases from other approved manufacturers or distributors?

These are just some of the questions that must be raised.

In the franchise industry, when a franchisor requires its franchisees to purchase products or equipment from it or an affiliate, it is known as a "tying arrangement". That is, the requirement to purchase the franchisor's products or equipment is "tied" to the purchase of the franchise. Some "tying arrangements" are very beneficial to franchisees, enabling them to purchase products and equipment at discounted prices or on an exclusive basis. Other "tying arrangements" can be the source of great conflict in a franchise system. The term "tying arrangement" is borrowed from the anti-trust field. It labels potentially illegal business arrangements where the holder of the rights to one service or product requires purchasers to also buy another product or service they may not necessarily want or desire, usually at above-market prices. Some franchisors have been charged with this practice when equipment, products or services must be purchased directly from the franchisor.

Are you able to purchase from other sources or are you required to purchase products or equipment only from the franchisor? Again, Item 8 of the UFOC should provide the answer. Although one of the reasons you may have joined the franchisor's system was to take advantage of buying power, a time may come when your own buying power or resources are better than those of the franchisor. Any opportunity you have to save money is obviously to your advantage. Having the ability to at least seek out alternative sources of supply and receive the franchisor's approval to purchase from that source is one way to ensure that you are not a shackled victim of a "tying arrangement". When possible, work to obtain flexibility within the system.

Review your contract carefully to determine the franchisor's purchasing requirements. This may include equipment and other items you will need to successfully operate your franchise outlet. It may also include future products and equipment developed by the franchisor. Make certain that your contract is clear on what the requirements are. The more surprises you can eliminate, the better prepared you will be for the future.

In some of the more popular and successful systems, franchisees have formed their own buying cooperatives, usually with the franchisor's approval. These cooperatives are established through either an established franchisee association or as the result of simple financial practicality. Lower costs are the primary feature for franchisees. Also, if the providers have been approved by the franchisor, it can be a welcome source of uniform quality control. Since franchisee-established cooperatives are normally voluntary and outside of the franchisor's offered package, new franchisees may only learn about the cooperative and its benefits by asking existing franchisees. Do not overlook this opportunity to find out more about the benefits one system may have over another.

OPERATIONS MANUALS
—THE HIDDEN AGREEMENT

Every franchise system should have an Operations Manual which franchisees must follow in conducting their business or risk termination. If the system does not have an Operations Manual it is a telltale sign of an ill-conceived or immature organization. Steer clear.

An Operations Manual should be the road map to conducting your new business. It may be the "textbook" used during your training classes, but that should not be the first time you see the manual. The UFOC Guidelines (Item 11) either require franchisors to make their Operations Manual available for review during the sales process or to set forth the Table of Contents in the Offering Circular. Too few purchasers take advantage of this opportunity. If they understood the importance of the manual, fewer would let the opportunity pass.

In essence, the manual is a continuation of the franchise agreement. It is specifically incorporated by reference into each franchise agreement. See Sections 6.7, 7.5 and 9.2.13 of the Franchise Agreement in the Appendix. Because franchisees are required to comply with the operations or procedures manual in the same way as the agreement itself, it must be reviewed with the same detail. Otherwise, it will represent a "hidden agreement" which may contain unfavorable and unworkable items.

Another feature of Operations Manual clauses to watch out for is the built-in "revisions clause" which permits the franchisor to revise the rules and the operations manual "from time to time." *This short phrase enables the franchisor to change the rules of the game whenever it wants to after the franchise agreement is signed.* Obviously, if the franchisor does not operate in good faith, this can mean unwanted system and product changes. *You should attempt to limit the changes the franchisor is allowed to make.* Since you can expect great resistance to negotiations in this area, this may be easier said than done. Nevertheless, inserting some general language that limits the franchisee's expenditures to make any change or which indicates that no revision will be made that alters the fundamental nature of franchise business, may provide some protection.

Be careful of the "hidden agreement". Take advantage of the chance to review the operations or procedures manual. It will give you greater insight into the franchise system as a whole and prevent unwanted surprises.

FRANCHISE TERRITORY

It is extremely important to have a thorough understanding of what your franchise agreement provides concerning the territory in which your franchise will be located. Item 12 of the Offering Circular usually spells out what you will receive.

Pay particular attention here. Many franchise systems do not provide an exclusive territory to new franchisees. You cannot assume that you are protected from having other franchisees or company-operated units placed in your marketing zone. This has become a very "hot" topic in franchising today.

It all started when one of the well-known hamburger chains began saturating markets with their locations. The same thing happened in the service station industry—when company-operated super-pumper stations began cropping up surprisingly close to dealer-operated locations of the same brand.

The franchising companies think of it as strategic-competitive marketing—displaying market dominance over other brands and competitors but franchisees and dealers view it as cannibalism, or as it has become better known—"encroachment." No other single topic has so dominated the franchising airwaves.

Encroachment can arise anytime a franchisee believes another system-unit is placed too close to an existing unit. This happens even when franchisees have no reserved or defined territory spelled out in their contracts. The better practice, although many franchisors refuse to grant them, is to always seek an exclusive, clearly defined territory.

A number of lawsuits have been brought against franchisors in the last few years. These have occurred mainly in the fast-food industry where competitive forces seem greatest. Franchisees have had limited success in the courtroom but have decidedly heightened the sensitivity of this issue. Unfortunately, this has been a double-edged sword.

While some franchisors have reacted positively by adopting specific policies and criteria to objectively identify and avoid potential encroachments, others have sharpened their contracts so no doubt exists that locations can be put side-by-side or on top of each other. New franchisees must be vigilant from the start.

Review the language on territorial rights and understand the risk you are taking. See Sections 1.2 and 21.2 of the Franchise Agreement in the Appendix. When possible, negotiate for a clearly defined territory. If not, inquire into the franchisor's policies. See if you can't at least get some reference in the contract to the general policy. Find out how other franchisees have coped with this issue.

DISPUTE RESOLUTION, CHOICE OF LAW AND FORUM SELECTION

Remember, when buying a franchise, start from the premise that the franchisor has spent hours writing the franchise agreement *for its own benefit.* One area where this is very obvious is the portion of the franchise agreement dealing with the resolution of disputes. Normally divided into several parts, the dispute resolution section of a franchise agreement is generally written to make sure that the franchisor controls how disputes are solved (e.g., arbitration, mediation, judicial), the law which will apply to the dispute (usually the franchisor's home state law), and where the dispute will be resolved (again, usually the franchisor's home state).

This is a difficult area for successful negotiation but it deserves attention. *Too often, even experienced franchisees are unaware of the way dispute resolution clauses can make it difficult or impossible to easily resolve a problem or sue their franchisor.* Many times, the effect of these clauses is not fully understood until after a dispute arises. This is usually too late. It is far better to understand the dispute resolution area of your franchise agreement before you sign it. Review Section 15 of the Franchise Agreement in the Appendix to determine what your rights would be.

Start by looking at the mechanism employed by the franchisor for the resolution of disputes. Are all disputes resolved by court action or is some form of "alternative dispute resolution" permitted? In the business world, a trend towards "alternative dispute resolution" has taken hold—that is, resolving disagreements out of court, generally through mediation or arbitration. The argument is that out-of-court resolution methods are superior to the judicial avenues because they are quicker, cheaper and more efficient. While alternative avenues to quick resolutions of disputes are worth looking at, each method must be evaluated *from the franchisee's viewpoint.*

For instance, arbitration is generally more favorable to franchise companies because franchise agreements usually mandate that arbitration occur in the franchisor's home city and state. Because of a special federal law that requires courts to strictly enforce arbitration clauses, the franchisor's selection of the place of arbitration is usually assured. If, on the other hand, the same selection was made in regard to a judicial forum, a court has more discretion to disregard the franchisor's selection. In addition, the arbitration process does not generally provide for pre-hearing/trial discovery. The discovery of information from the franchisor's records and employees—to substantiate certain claims made by the franchisee—can be crucial to the success of the case. Finally, arbitration provisions can be used to squelch class action suits brought by disgruntled franchisees. *This feature is of such paramount importance to the franchisor that it is unlikely to grant any change regarding it.*

Not all arbitration proposals should be rejected out of hand, however. *Arbitration tends to be cheaper and faster than litigation in court.* But, is it a good idea to be forced to arbitrate immediately rather than allowing the parties to decide after a dispute arises? And why can't arbitration occur in the franchisee's city? *The franchisee generally has a lot less money than the franchisor and, accordingly, will find it more burdensome to travel to another location to resolve a dispute.*

Franchise companies also try to control the law that will apply to a dispute or a violation of state law. This is a significant area. By mandating (making sure) their home state laws apply to the relationship, franchisors can limit claims brought under the franchisee's home state franchise protection laws. And further, a quirk in many state laws does not allow an out-of-state franchise purchaser to bring a claim under the franchisor's state law because many of the laws apply to resident purchasers or operators only. In essence, this allows franchisors to nullify franchisee claims that would be valid under another state's law, if they had not agreed to the choice of law clause in the franchise agreement.

Another area to keep your eye on is "jury waiver". That is a clause that gives up your right to trial before a jury. You should attempt to preserve your right to present your dispute to a jury of your peers.

Justifing it under the banner of uniformity, franchisors generally employ another obstacle to franchisee friendly resolution of franchise disputes: forum selection clauses. These clauses require franchisees to bring any arbitration or court action in the franchise company's hometown. The primary reasons for this are to make it more expensive for franchisees to bring an action, allow the franchisor to use their hometown lawyers and take advantage of whatever goodwill the company may have developed in the local community. The end result is to discourage franchisees from bringing legal actions to resolve disputes and violations of the law.

Another real life example demonstrates the disadvantage franchisees can face when a dispute arises. Our shipping clerk, who was introduced earlier, incurred great expense fighting with her franchisor, only to exhaust all of her resources before her day in court arrived. Here's what happened:

Some evidence of franchisor misrepresentation was discovered. The personnel placement business did not take-off as expected. Our franchisee felt she was entitled to the money she paid the franchisor as well as what she generally invested in the failing business. Suit was filed in state court in her home state, Indiana (the franchising company was located in Arizona).

At the time, Indiana had a favorable franchise law that the franchisee claimed was violated and entitled her to all of her damages. The franchise agreement said the law of Arizona would apply, any suit or arbitration must be brought in Arizona and that all disputes brought by the franchisee were subject to arbitration. Arizona had no special franchise law.

The first move by the franchise company was to remove the case from the state court into an Indiana federal court. The next was to transfer the case to an Arizona federal court in its home district. (Our shipping clerk now had to hire a second lawyer in Arizona.) Once there, the franchise company demanded that the federal court order the case to arbitration, which it did. As a parting shot, the franchisor was able to convince the court that the entire arbitration should be controlled by Arizona law, Indiana law would not apply.

While the franchisee fought gallantly at each turn—having unsuccessfully opposed three preliminary but devastating motions, hiring two lawyers, and being dragged half way across the country—she had about all she could take. She was out of money. The franchisor won because she could not continue. She closed her business and went looking for the bankruptcy court.

As is recommended with any unfavorable advantage a franchisor may have, you should seek to soften the effect of these clauses through negotiation. Failing that, you should have a clear understanding of these dispute resolution clauses before you sign the agreement or, at a minimum, before a dispute arises. The dispute resolution clauses can have a dramatic effect on the outcome of the dispute.

To sum up, negotiating the contract with the franchisor can be complex, fruitful, and frustrating. However, do not hesitate to at least try to strike the best bargain you can. Even though you are aware that an imbalance exists, the way to right it is to enter into negotiations with the idea that everything is negotiable. You may surprise yourself. *Remember, it never hurts to ask.*

13

YOUR RELATIONSHIP WITH THE FRANCHISOR

Do not underestimate the importance of your relationship with the franchisor. You do not join a franchising system to operate your business in a vacuum. You pay a franchise fee to benefit from the experience of the franchisor. Expect it. Demand it. In a general sense, the franchise fee is payment for the franchisor's experience. Remember this, and make sure that you get your money's worth.

Opening the doors to your new business is an exciting experience that will, at first, consume you with the details of its day-to-day operation. While this will be physically, emotionally, and psychologically draining, you should begin monitoring your relationship with the franchisor immediately.

By tracking the assistance and services you get against what was promised by the franchisor, you can systematically assess the franchisor's performance. Make a list of all the services promised to you in your franchise agreement. Within the first three to six months of your opening, determine if the promised services have been delivered, whether your questions and needs are addressed promptly, and whether the franchise system runs smoothly and effectively.

Before you even open your doors, you will probably participate in the franchisor's training program. The training program is your window on the quality of the franchise system and a good time to begin the monitoring process. First impressions are important. Was the training program conducted in an organized and thorough fashion? The answer to this question may give you some insight into things to come. The training program is your first real opportunity to evaluate the franchisor's performance. Let's go back to our ill-fated shipping clerk.

Her first suspicion surfaced during training. Her training experience was very haphazard. The instructors did not know their material well. There were many "holes" in the program, resulting in unproductive downtime. It appeared that the training was being offered for the first time. One of the misrepresentations later discovered was that, although the franchisor appeared to have a solid track record, its outlets, represented as franchisees, were actually independent operators who were drawn into the franchisor's system after they had opened independently and thought it was a good idea to band together under a common trademark. As it turned out this was the first time the franchisor was actually training anyone and the shipping clerk was the first real franchisee!

Trust your instincts. Because the operation of a franchise system involves a partnership between you and the parent company, the franchisor's performance is an important ingredient.

In addition to training and general supervisory assistance, you will probably expect the franchisor to help with "opening day" promotion, assistance with accounting systems, advertising, inventory control, employee evaluation and training, and general management direction. As we discussed earlier, any assistance that you expect to receive should be spelled out in the contract.

Don't wait till opening day to find out what you should have written into the contract.

The franchise company, especially within the first six months to one year, should be extremely eager to help you succeed with your business. If this assistance is not forthcoming, you should immediately notify the company in writing. Before you complain though, check the promises in your contract. What did the franchisor agree to do? Distinguish "may" clauses from "shall" clauses, just as you did when you reviewed the contract. Make sure you have the ammunition to back-up your claim. If you don't find support in the contract itself, does any of the franchisor's promotional information tout the services it promises to provide? Look for something in writing.

Be constructive with your complaints and set realistic deadlines for the requested performance. It will be important at this stage to maintain thorough and complete records of your communications with the franchisor. If the situation deteriorates, and can later only be resolved by litigation or arbitration, your written notifications and communications will be crucial to any recovery. Keeping a checklist of expected services and the franchisor's performance is a good way to preserve your communications and realize your expectations.

If your communication of dissatisfaction is of no avail, and you are obligated to make royalty payments under the terms of your franchise agreement, an effective, but clearly risky way to communicate your dissatisfaction is to withhold royalty payments. The risk is that withholding royalty payments is a violation of your franchise agreement. The franchisor may seize upon this opportunity to declare your agreement terminated. So withholding royalty payments should be used only as a last resort. Many courts have upheld franchise terminations based on failure to pay royalties, even when the franchisee had seemingly good reasons for doing so. Of course, in some situations, it may be the only way to get the attention of a recalcitrant franchisor.

If you find it necessary to withhold royalties, the better practice is to inform the franchisor in writing in advance and arrange an "escrowing" of the payments with a third-party, such as your attorney or banker. Or, even better, seek a court order allowing you to pay the royalties into a court escrow during the resolution of the dispute. This way, if the franchisor pursues the drastic remedy of attempted termination, you will be prepared to show your good faith by continuing your royalty payments in spite of your disagreement.

Beyond monitoring the basics of your relationship with the franchisor, you should also analyze the methods and avenues available for your input into the franchisor's system. This input, and the input of other franchisees, may enhance your business as well as the franchisor's. If you find your—or other franchisees' —ideas and suggestions for improving the franchise falling on the franchisor's deaf ears, you should do your best to correct this problem. (More on this in the next chapter.)

If you experience serious problems with lack of support, you should consult your attorney to discuss various approaches to the problem. For instance, assessing the risks of withholding royalties. Hopefully, when the franchisor realizes that you are serious about getting professional help, they will become responsive to your situation.

14

FRANCHISEE INPUT AND FRANCHISEE ASSOCIATIONS

No product or service, no matter how good, can maintain its lasting power without new ideas and constant improvement.

Your franchisor has presented you with an idea. Hopefully, it has a tested format and a proven track record. But will it continue to be successful in the future or at least as long as the term of your franchise agreement?

The longevity of a franchising system can be influenced and prolonged by the direct involvement of the franchisees. Franchisees can play a vital role in improving the franchise system. Finding a franchise system that caters to franchisee input is fundamental. Working within a franchise system that has not evolved to this stage can be frustrating, but not altogether hopeless. If the channels for basic communication have not been forged in your system, work constructively to do so. If they exist and are used effectively, take advantage of the opportunity.

Franchisees, through their day-to-day operation of the business, will become aware of product information, delivery of service, and other minor but important details which may escape the attention of the franchisor. In addition, franchisees may become aware of more efficient and economical ways of providing the delivered product or service.

From this, you can see that it is important for everyone in the system to communicate and have a forum for a healthy exchange of ideas. The franchisor who does not seek the input of franchisees is making a drastic mistake. And, franchisees who make no effort to get the franchisor to understand this, have only themselves to blame.

FRANCHISEE COUNCILS

Part of your initial investigation should focus on franchisee input in the franchise system. Some franchise companies conduct annual meetings where franchisees have the opportunity to exchange information with the company and their fellow franchisees. While annual meetings can be productive experiences, too many are window-dressing, barely scratching the surface of system problems. Some franchisors misuse the annual meeting opportunity by hyping the purported success of the system and offering the "company viewpoint" rather than creating an atmosphere for honest, effective communication.

To accomplish effective channels for two-way communication, some systems have established Franchisee Councils which are composed of appointed or elected franchisee-representatives and liaisons from the franchisor. The councils meet on a regular basis to exchange information, discuss the development or presentation of new products and services, and critique the franchisor and franchisee performance. In addition, the councils serve an important, everyday function needed in every large organization: a healthy avenue to vent frustration or disapproval of system-wide issues and problems. The availability of the franchisee council can mean all the difference in the world when sensitive issues arise.

FRANCHISEE ASSOCIATIONS

No discussion of franchising would be complete without touching on franchisee associations. Ten years ago when the first edition of this book appeared, it ended with the prediction that "there will logically come a time in the foreseeable future when there will be industry-wide and nationwide franchisees' associations formed to protect their particular interests in the franchising system". That prediction has become reality. And, the emergence of these franchisee-associations have changed the dynamics of the franchising industry.

Historically, the only viable franchising association was the franchisor-controlled IFA. While the IFA produced educational information for franchise purchasers and offered other informational services on franchising, its main mission was to lobby Congress, the FTC and state legislatures on behalf of franchisors. It generally opposed laws protecting franchisees and franchise buyers. All this changed when a favorable pro-franchisee law was passed in Iowa, and two franchisee associations arrived on the scene: The American Association of Franchisees and Dealers and the American Franchisee Association. Both associations, mentioned in the resource section at the beginning of this book, have had a strong impact on the franchising community. Their emergence, and a sentiment that the Iowa law marked a national trend towards stronger franchisee legislation, forced a change in the structure of the IFA.

The exclusive franchisor-IFA club started accepting franchisee-members in an effort to forge a trade association that spoke for all of frachising, seeking to effectively balance the interests of franchisor and franchisee alike. This change in course was accompanied by a commensurate change in philosophy—the IFA adopted a Code of Principles and Standards that set out certain franchisee-oriented guidelines franchisors should follow. In its lobbying role, the IFA would take a middle course in areas of franchisor-franchisee conflict and focus on issues of mutual interest.

Although The American Association of Franchisees and Dealers and the American Franchisee Association would like to take full credit for this turn of events, in addition to the Iowa law, another dynamic was at play. Congressman John J. La Falce, Chairman of the House of Representatives Committee on Small Business, was pressuring the IFA and franchisors with proposals to adopt national legislation offering franchisees more protection during the franchise relationship—focusing on some controversial matters such as encroachment on franchisees' territories and restrictions on the termination of franchise agreements.

Many have been skeptical of the IFA's motives in admitting franchisee members, and internal disputes within the organization suggest that all are still not comfortable with the change. The philisophical change has come with the speed of turning an oil tanker around but the ultimate objective of the IFA is to represent the best of franchising practices. Regardless of whether true change has come about in the IFA, the effect the new franchisee associations have had on the frachise community is striking.

The American Association of Franchisees and Dealers and the American Franchisee Association have different approaches and goals but share the mission of helping franchisees and franchise buyers. Contact them at the addresses or telephone numbers given at the beginning of the book to learn about their membership opportunities and educational information. Both associations have been active in lobbying governmental agencies on behalf of franchisees and, through their own methods, working with franchisors to bring greater balance to the franchise relationship. In addition, both groups frequently offer or participate in educational seminars made available to franchisees and franchise buyers.

Take advantage of the resources offered by the three major franchise associations. At the buying stage, the background and philosophy of the groups is much less important than the information and guidance they have to offer. Later, after you have entered the ranks of your fellow franchisees, if you believe your interests are served by joining a franchisee association, you can select the group right for you.

A strong, established association of franchise owners, whether organized through the resources of an outside franchisee association or the determination of fellow franchisees, is a positive force in a franchise system's dynamics. Many times, a unified association of franchisees brings the strength and negotiating power that no single franchisee can achieve. As franchise systems mature, and growing pains turn to disputes, a solid franchisee association can make all of the difference in the world.

Franchisee associations, especially when they come about before problems arise, can serve many roles with the franchisor: advisor; mediator; persuader; and group negotiator. By establishing a good relationship early, a franchisee association can have effective impact at the most crucial times. Working constructively with the franchisor, and establishing a reliable reputation before material issues arise, poises the association for influential input when crisis arise.

When buying a franchise look for this important attribute. Find out what involvement and impact the franchisee council or association has. If your system does not have an established council or association, find out why not. If you need help in getting one off the ground, contact one of the major franchisee associations for assistance in organizing one. Everyone will be better off—and your franchisor may someday thank you for the effort.

CONCLUSION

Franchising offers a great opportunity for both franchisors and franchisees. It brings together the concentrated power of corporate America and the more diffuse power of small business. It runs on the basic principles of hard work and reward for one's efforts. This blend of entrepreneurial forces makes it an extremely successful method of doing business. As we have learned, however, success is not guaranteed. Careful independent analysis must precede any franchise purchase. Exercising caution and good business sense is imperative. Diving into the franchising pool without first checking how deep the water is can result in disastrous consequences. Look before you leap!

The FTC, NASAA, and a number of states have given franchise buyers effective, valuable tools not available to their predecessors. Registration, disclosure documents and general protective measures allow present day buyers to make informed decisions. Resources available through the Internet, franchise associations and government agencies provide an added edge. As a whole, today's franchise buyers are better able to find the right franchise system than in the past. Although not completely corrected, the "informational imbalance" that plagued early franchise purchasers has been somewhat leveled.

It is the franchise buyer's responsibility to conduct a thorough and deliberate search for the right franchise partner. Many existing franchise systems offer a variety of excellent choices.

Some are more popular, some more expensive, others are new, upcoming ventures. Whatever the industry, whatever the product or service, the educated entrepreneur will conduct a systematic search to select the best franchise system that their money can buy.

Following a thorough investigation, the franchise buyer must be prepared to accept the franchisor's agreement or develop a realistic negotiation strategy. Clarifying major points of the franchise agreement is an important threshold event. Evaluate where your leverage may lie and attempt to negotiate onerous provisions to your favor. Never pass up the opportunity to negotiate the franchise contract.

Franchisees play a vital and fundamental role in improving the system. Finding a system that welcomes franchisee input is a sign of a bright future. Unfortunately not all franchise organizations have evolved to this point. Work constructively with your franchisor to bring meaningful input to your new system.

Your patient analysis of the available franchise systems will pay large dividends. Do not decide too quickly. Develop a system and stick to it. Draw upon the knowledge and wisdom of your professional advisors. Dot all the "i's" and cross all the "t's" in the franchise agreement—it is your only chance. We wish you the best of luck with your franchising endeavors, and we hope you will heed the advice in this book and never permit luck to replace careful inquiry.

A

SAMPLE UNIFORM FRANCHISE OFFERING CIRCULAR

(Some Material Deleted)

[Registered Trademark or Service Mark] **Appears Here**

No. _____

FRANCHISE OFFERING CIRCULAR
FOR PROSPECTIVE FRANCHISEES
AS REQUIRED BY THE STATE OF _____

XYZ, Inc.
(COMPANY NAME, ADDRESS,
AND TELEPHONE NUMBER)

XYZ Franchise Corp. offers two approaches for the acquisition of an XYZ Pogo Sticks store franchise. You may acquire the right to open and operate multiple XYZ Pogo Sticks stores within a specific geographic area by executing a XYZ Development Agreement, or you may acquire the right to open a single XYZ Pogo Sticks store under an individual XYZ Franchise Agreement.

In both approaches, the franchise offered by XYZ Franchise Corp. is a nonexclusive right and license to be an XYZ Franchisee, to own and operate an XYZ Pogo Sticks store and to the use of the XYZ Operating System, together with the service marks, trade names, and other techniques and business systems utilized in the operation of XYZ Pogo Sticks stores.

The Development Fee required under the Development Agreement will vary, and is determined by multiplying the number of Pogo Sticks stores to be opened and operated within the specified Development Area by $_____. The initial Franchise Fee required under the Franchise Agreement is $_____.

The Development Fee is applied to reduce the Franchise Fee by $_____ for each Pogo Sticks store opened within the Territory. The Franchise Fee is generally nonrefundable, except as provided in Item 5.

The estimated initial investment required by you for a single XYZ Pogo Sticks store, including the initial Development Fee and Franchise Fee for a single location, will range from $_____ to $_____. This amount does not represent your total investment in connection with the XYZ Franchise. Items 5 to 7 of this Offering Circular should be consulted for further explanation regarding the total investment.

RISK FACTORS

1. THE FRANCHISE AGREEMENT PERMITS YOU TO SUE OR ARBITRATE ONLY IN _____. OUT OF STATE LITIGATION OR ARBITRATION MAY FORCE YOU TO ACCEPT A LESS FAVORABLE SETTLEMENT FOR DISPUTES. IT MAY ALSO COST MORE TO SUE OR ARBITRATE IN _____ THAN IN YOUR HOME STATE.

2. THE FRANCHISE AGREEMENT STATES THAT
_____ LAW GOVERNS THE AGREEMENT, AND
THIS LAW MAY NOT PROVIDE THE SAME PRO-
TECTIONS AND BENEFITS AS LOCAL LAW. YOU
MAY WANT TO COMPARE THESE LAWS.
3. THERE MAY BE OTHER RISKS CONCERNING THIS
FRANCHISE.

INFORMATION ABOUT COMPARISONS OF FRAN-
CHISORS IS AVAILABLE. CALL THE STATE ADMINIS-
TRATORS LISTED IN EXHIBIT ___ OR YOUR PUBLIC
LIBRARY FOR SOURCES OF INFORMATION.

REGISTRATION OF THIS FRANCHISE WITH ANY
STATE DOES NOT MEAN THAT THE STATE RECOM-
MENDS IT OR HAS VERIFIED THE INFORMATION IN
THIS OFFERING CIRCULAR. IF YOU LEARN THAT
ANY THING IN THIS OFFERING CIRCULAR IS
UNTRUE, CONTACT THE FEDERAL TRADE COMMIS-
SION.

EFFECTIVE DATE:_____

THIS OFFERING CIRCULAR IS PROVIDED FOR YOUR
OWN PROTECTION AND CONTAINS A SUMMARY
ONLY OF CERTAIN MATERIAL PROVISIONS OF THE
FRANCHISE AGREEMENT. THIS OFFERING CIRCU-
LAR AND ALL CONTRACTS OR AGREEMENTS
SHOULD BE READ CAREFULLY IN THEIR ENTIRETY
FOR AN UNDERSTANDING OF ALL RIGHTS AND
OBLIGATIONS OF BOTH XYZ FRANCHISE CORP. AND
YOU.

A FEDERAL TRADE COMMISSION RULE MAKES IT
UNLAWFUL TO OFFER OR SELL ANY FRANCHISE

WITHOUT FIRST PROVIDING THIS OFFERING CIR-
CULAR TO THE PROSPECTIVE FRANCHISEE AT THE
EARLIER OF (1) THE FIRST PERSONAL MEETING OR;
(2) 10 BUSINESS DAYS BEFORE THE SIGNING OF ANY
FRANCHISE OR RELATED AGREEMENT OR; (3) 10
BUSINESS DAYS BEFORE ANY PAYMENT. PROSPEC-
TIVE FRANCHISEES MUST ALSO RECEIVE A FRAN-
CHISE AGREEMENT CONTAINING ALL MATERIAL
TERMS AT LEAST FIVE BUSINESS DAYS PRIOR TO
THE SIGNING OF THE FRANCHISE AGREEMENT.

IF THIS OFFERING CIRCULAR IS NOT DELIVERED
ON TIME, OR IF IT CONTAINS A FALSE, INCOM-
PLETE, INACCURATE, OR MISLEADING STATEMENT,
A VIOLATION OF FEDERAL AND STATE LAW MAY
HAVE OCCURRED AND SHOULD BE REPORTED TO
THE FEDERAL TRADE COMMISSION, WASHINGTON,
D.C. 20580.

The name and address of the Franchisor's Agent in the State
of_____authorized to receive service of process is:

_____

_____

DISCLOSURE DOCUMENT FOR PROSPECTIVE FRANCHISEES

FRANCHISOR:
[Company Name, Address and Telephone Number]

INFORMATION FOR PROSPECTIVE FRANCHISEES REQUIRED BY FEDERAL TRADE COMMISSION

• • •

TO PROTECT YOU, WE HAVE REQUIRED YOUR FRANCHISOR TO GIVE YOU THIS INFORMATION. WE HAVE NOT CHECKED IT, AND DO NOT KNOW IF IT IS CORRECT. IT SHOULD HELP YOU MAKE UP YOUR MIND. STUDY IT CAREFULLY. WHILE IT INCLUDES SOME INFORMATION ABOUT YOUR CONTRACT, DO NOT RELY ON IT ALONE TO UNDERSTAND YOUR CONTRACT. READ ALL OF YOUR CONTRACT CAREFULLY. BUYING A FRANCHISE IS A COMPLICATED INVESTMENT. TAKE YOUR TIME TO DECIDE. IF POSSIBLE, SHOW YOUR CONTRACT AND THIS INFORMATION TO AN ADVISOR, LIKE A LAWYER OR AN ACCOUNTANT. IF YOU FIND ANYTHING YOU THINK MAY BE WRONG OR ANYTHING IMPORTANT THAT HAS BEEN LEFT OUT, YOU SHOULD LET US KNOW ABOUT IT. IT MAY BE AGAINST THE LAW.

THERE MAY ALSO BE LAWS ON FRANCHISING IN YOUR STATE. ASK YOUR STATE AGENCIES ABOUT THEM.

FEDERAL TRADE COMMISSION
WASHINGTON, D.C. 20580

DATE OF THIS DISCLOSURE IS:

TABLE OF CONTENTS

ITEM   **PAGE**

ITEM 1   THE FRANCHISOR, ITS
         PREDECESSORS AND AFFILIATES 153

ITEM 2   BUSINESS EXPERIENCE 156

ITEM 3   LITIGATION 157

ITEM 4   BANKRUPTCY 157

ITEM 5   INITIAL FRANCHISE FEE 157

ITEM 6   OTHER FEES 159

ITEM 7   FRANCHISEE'S INITIAL
         INVESTMENT 161

ITEM 8   RESTRICTIONS ON SOURCES OF
         PRODUCTS AND SERVICES 163

ITEM 9   FRANCHISEE'S OBLIGATIONS 165

ITEM 10 FINANCING 166

ITEM 11 FRANCHISOR'S OBLIGATIONS 166

ITEM 12 TERRITORY 176

ITEM 13 TRADEMARKS 178

ITEM 14 PATENTS, COPYRIGHTS, AND PROPRI-
         ETARY INFORMATION 180

ITEM 15   OBLIGATION TO PARTICIPATE IN THE
          ACTUAL OPERATION OF THE FRANCHISE
          BUSINESS   180

ITEM 16   RESTRICTIONS ON WHAT FRANCHISEE
          MAY SELL   181

ITEM 17   RENEWAL, TERMINATION, TRANSFER,
          AND DISPUTE RESOLUTION   181

ITEM 18   PUBLIC FIGURES   182

ITEM 19   EARNINGS CLAIMS   183

ITEM 20   LIST OF OUTLETS   183

ITEM 21   FINANCIAL STATEMENTS   183

ITEM 22   CONTRACTS   184

ITEM 23   RECEIPT   184

EXHIBITS

A. XYZ Franchise Corp. Development Agreement
B. XYZ Franchise Corp. Franchise Agreement
C. Information Regarding Earnings Capability of XYZ, Franchise Corp.'s Franchisees
D. Financial Statements of XYZ Franchise Corp.
E. Information Regarding Franchisees of XYZ Franchise Corp.
F. List of State Administrators
G. Training Outline
H. Receipt

ITEM 1
THE FRANCHISOR, ITS PREDECESSOR
AND AFFILIATES

To simplify the language in this Offering Circular, "XYZ International" means XYZ International Franchise Corp., "XYZ" means XYZ, Inc., and "you" means the person or entity (and the owners of the entity) who purchases the franchise. This Franchise Offering is made by XYZ to prospective, qualified Franchisees (as defined below). XYZ International's predecessor is XYZ Franchise Corporation, which was incorporated on _____ [date], and commenced business operations on _____ [date]. XYZ Franchise Corporation never operated an XYZ Pogo Sticks store. It has never operated businesses other than as are related to the franchising of XYZ Pogo Sticks stores. However, XYZ-USA Inc., the parent of XYZ Franchise Corporation, has operated similar businesses under the trade name XYZ since _____[date], through various affiliated corporations and partnerships. On _____[date], XYZ International purchased the assets of XYZ Franchise Corporation. XYZ International was specifically incorporated on _____[date], for the purpose of acquiring all the assets of XYZ Franchise Corporation and the XYZ Franchise System. XYZ International does business under the names "XYZ _____," "_____," and "_____." XYZ International's, its predecessor's, and affiliates' principal business address is _____. XYZ International's agent for service of process is identified on page _____ above. XYZ International is a [state] corporation. XYZ International is a wholly owned subsidiary of XYZ International, Inc., a [state] corporation, which was formerly known as XYZ/ABC, Inc. Upon the formation of XYZ International, XYZ/ABC, Inc. changed its name to XYZ International, Inc. XYZ Pogo Sticks stores (sometimes individually referred to herein as the "Pogo Sticks stores") are businesses devoted to entertainment outside of the home and are used primarily by the general public. XYZ International does not operate a XYZ Pogo Sticks store similar to the Pogo Sticks stores being offered to you. XYZ International is not involved in the operation of any other business.

The rights and franchise offered by XYZ in this state are contained in two basic documents: the Development Agreement and the Franchise Agreement. You must first execute a Development Agreement, which reserves a specific geographic territory (the "Territory") in which to open and operate XYZ Pogo Sticks stores.

The Development Agreement grants you the exclusive right to select proposed sites for XYZ Pogo Sticks stores within the Territory, and, upon acceptance of a proposed site by XYZ, to enter into a Franchise Agreement with XYZ to enable you to construct, open, and operate a XYZ Pogo Sticks store upon that site. The Development Agreement provides for the construction and opening of a fixed number of XYZ Pogo Sticks stores in the Territory in accordance with a development and performance time schedule (the "Development Schedule"). The number of Pogo Sticks stores and the Development Schedule are agreed upon by you and XYZ before the execution of the Development Agreement, and are based upon such considerations as geographic size and population of the area, economic and demographic statistics, and your prior business experience.

At the same time as or shortly after your execution of the Development Agreement, you and XYZ must enter into a Franchise Agreement. You receive the right to construct, own and operate an XYZ Pogo Sticks store at that site and to use XYZ's system for providing products and services, including standards, specifications and methods, procedures, techniques, management directives, identification schemes and proprietary marks. If your Development Agreement is for multiple Pogo Sticks stores, you and XYZ must enter into separate franchise agreements for each site.

XYZ commenced selling XYZ Franchises upon its incorporation and acquisition of the assets of XYZ Franchise Corporation on _____ [date].

The Pogo Sticks store industry is heavily regulated. You should familiarize yourself with the regulations that apply to the operation of a Pogo Sticks store in your state and locale. Many laws and regulations that apply to businesses generally also apply to Pogo Sticks stores: American With Disabilities Act, Federal Wage and Hour Laws and the Occupational Health and Safety Act.

The Pogo Sticks store business is highly competitive and is affected by the competition in your area. You will compete with other retail establishments, some of which will be national chains, franchise establishments and locally-based Pogo Sticks stores offering similar items. You should make every effort to investigate the competition in your area.

ITEM 2
BUSINESS EXPERIENCE

President, Director: ABRAHAM ADAMS

On _____, Mr. Adams was elected to the Board of Directors of XYZ International and appointed President. On_____, Mr. Adams was elected President and a Director of XYZ and served in those capacities until the formation of XYZ International. Before the formation of XYZ, Mr. Adams was elected President of _____ and continues to serve in that capacity. All of these positions were held in East Island, New Jersey.

Senior Vice President, Secretary and Director:
BRIAN BIGGS

On _____, Mr. Biggs was elected to the Board of Directors of XYZ International and appointed Secretary and Senior Vice President. Shortly after_____, Mr. Biggs was elected Secretary, Treasurer and a Director of XYZ-ABC and served in those capacities until the formation of XYZ International. He also served as Vice-President of Development of XYZ-ABC during its existence. Before the formation of XYZ-ABC, Mr. Biggs was Vice President of Development of XYZ Management commencing in _____ and serving in that capacity until _____. All of these positions were in East Island, New Jersey.

Chief Financial Officer, Treasurer and Director:
CYRIL CEE

On _____, Mr. Cee was elected to the Board of Directors of XYZ International and appointed Treasurer and Chief Financial Officer. Mr. Cee joined XYZ-ABC as Chief Financial Officer in _____, was elected to the Board of Directors in _____ and served in those capacities until the formation of XYZ International. All of these positions were in East Island, New Jersey. From _____, Mr. Cee was a member of the professional staff of the CDE Accounting Firm, serving most recently as Accounting Supervisor where he worked with various privately-held and publicly-held companies, primarily in the scrap iron industry.

ITEM 3
LITIGATION

No litigation is required to be disclosed in this Offering.

[DISCLOSURE MUST BE MADE OF ANY PENDING ADMINISTRATIVE, CRIMINAL OR MATERIAL CIVIL ACTION ALLEGING VIOLATIONS OF A FRANCHISE, ANTITRUST OR SECURITIES LAW, FRAUD, OR UNFAIR OR DECEPTIVE PRACTICES AS WELL AS ANY JUDGMENT DURING THE LAST TEN YEARS INVOLVING THE SAME].

ITEM 4
BANKRUPTCY

No person previously identified in Items 1 or 2 of this Offering Circular has been involved as a debtor in proceedings under the U.S. Bankruptcy Code required to be disclosed in this Item.

ITEM 5
INITIAL FRANCHISE FEE

Upon execution of the Development Agreement, you must pay an amount to XYZ as consideration for XYZ's reservation of the Territory for you (the "Development Fee"). This amount is determined by multiplying the number of XYZ's Pogo Sticks stores to be opened in the Territory by $_____. The Development Fee is due upon signing of the Development Agreement. The Development Fee is applied to reduce the Franchise Fee, described below, by $_____ for each Pogo Sticks store opened in the Territory.

In addition, and in situations where no Development Agreement has been executed, you must pay an initial Franchise Fee of $_____ for a single XYZ Pogo Sticks store location, which is due from you upon the signing of the Franchise Agreement.

The Franchise Fee, less $_____ for training expenses incurred by XYZ, will be refunded to you if XYZ declines to approve your principal owner(s) and management staff as having successfully completed all of the components of XYZ's Initial Training Program. Before a refund is made, you must return all Manuals and other materials provided to you and your employees, and execute a Mutual Release in which you and XYZ release each other from all liabilities or obligations imposed by Franchise Agreement, except for the Confidentiality and Nondisclosure and Noncompetition provisions of that Agreement. The Franchise Fee under all other circumstances are nonrefundable.

Except as stated above, proceeds of the Development Fee and the Franchise Fee are nonrefundable, are not specifically allocated, and are, in part, income to XYZ and, are, in part, used to pay various expenses and costs of XYZ.

ITEM 6
OTHER FEES

Name of Fee (1)	Amount	Due Date	Remarks
Royalty Fee	___% of total gross sales (2)	Payable weekly beginning with the first week, or any portion of any week, the Pogo Sticks store is open for business	Payable on the first Tuesday after each calendar week
Interest on Unpaid Royalty Fees	_____% per month on amount owed	First day of the week following the week in which the Royalty Fee payment is due	Payable on demand. Interest rate cannot exceed the maximum interest rate permitted by applicable law (3)
Advertising Fees	_____% of total monthly gross sales	On-going monthly expense	Paid directly by you to third party
Advertising Fees (National Fund)	Up to___% of total monthly gross sales	On-going monthly expense (when established)	Directed to XYZ National Fund (4)
Advertising Fees	_____% total gross sales	Payable weekly at the time Royalty Fees are paid	Directed to XYZ International's Production and Marketing Fund (5)
Advertising Fees	$_____ to $ _____	Before and at time of opening the Pogo Sticks store	Local advertising and promotion as required by XYZ International
Administrative Assignment Fee	$_____ for the Development Agreement and $_____ for each Franchise Agreement	Before effectiveness of the assignment	Applies when you sell or otherwise transfer your rights under an Agreement

Name of Fee(1)	Amount	Due Date	Remarks
Training Fee			
Initial	No training fee, however, you bear certain expenses for your employees	As incurred	Expenses include travel, lodging and wages payable or incurred in training your employees
Audit Fee			
No under-payment	None	N/A	If no underpayment is found, you bear no cost of XYZ International's expenses
Underpayment of 2% or less	Amount of each underpayment plus 1-1/2% interest on each amount underpaid until paid	Immediately upon determination	Applies to Royalty Fees, contributions to XYZ International's Production and Marketing Fund, or any other amounts payable under the Franchise Agreement
Underpayment over 2%	Amount of each underpayment plus 1-1/2% interest on each amount underpaid until paid and all XYZ International's expenses actually incurred in the audit and correction	Immediately upon determination	Applies to Royalty Fees, contributions to XYZ International's Production and Marketing Fund, and any other amounts payable under the Franchise Agreement

NOTES:

1. The fees listed in this chart are not refundable.
2. "Gross sales" means all sums you receive for all sales, merchandise and all business transacted from the premises of the Pogo Sticks store, including off-premises catering, but does not include bona fide refunds and credits for

returns of merchandise or the amounts paid for any sales tax, retailers occupation tax, or other tax.

3. You shall also deliver a monthly report to XYZ International by the 25th day of each month in the form of an Operating Statement of Receipts, Disbursements and an Aged Summary of Accounts Payable, and Marketing Report for the last calendar month.

4. The national advertising fund promotes and advertises the XYZ Franchise System. It may be established at any time and a charge of up to 2% of monthly gross sales may be assessed.

5. The Production and Marketing Fund prepares and produces advertising materials and ad copy which can be used by you and other franchisees to advertise your XYZ Pogo Sticks store. You may obtain an accounting of Production and Marketing Fund expenditures by requesting the same from XYZ International. The Production and Marketing Fund promotes XYZ Pogo Sticks stores generally through advertising or marketing media. You may obtain an accounting of Production and Marketing Fund expenditures by requesting it from XYZ International.

ITEM 7
FRANCHISEE'S INITIAL INVESTMENT

The following table represents an estimate of the initial investment you can expect to make if you open a single Pogo Sticks store:

YOUR ESTIMATED INITIAL INVESTMENT

Expense	Amount	Method of Payment	When Due	To Whom Payment is Made
Initial Franchise Fee (See Note 1)	$_____	Lump Sum	Signing of Franchise Agreement	XYZ
Traveling and Living Expenses During Training	$_____ to _____	As Incurred	Before Opening	Airlines, Hotels, and Pogo Sticks stores

Expense	Amount	Method of Payment	When Due	To Whom Payment is Made
Real Estate Leased (See Note 2)	$_____ to _____ per month	As Incurred	During Lease	Landlord
Equipment (See Note 3)	$_____ to _____	Lump Sum	Before Opening	Equipment Suppliers and Office Supply Companies
Leasehold Improvements	$_____ to _____	Lump Sum	Before Opening	Contractor
Lease and Utility Deposits	$_____	Lump Sum	Before Opening	Landlord and Utility Companies
Furniture and Fixtures	$_____ to _____	Lump Sum	Before Opening	Various Suppliers
Initial Software	$_____	Lump Sum	Before Opening	Software Vendors
General Office Supplies	$_____ to _____	Lump Sum	Before Opening	Various Suppliers
Insurance	$_____	Lump Sum	Annual Premium	Insurance Company or Agent
Additional Funds –6 Months (See Note 4)	$_____ to _____	As Incurred	As Incurred	Employees, Suppliers, Utilities, Etc.

TOTAL $ _____ to _____ (See Note 5) (Does Not Include Ongoing Rent.)

(The amount of cost estimates are based on purchasing the items with one hundred percent (100%) cash payments. The estimated initial investment may be lower if alternative means of financing and/or purchasing are utilized by you.)

NOTES

NOTE 1: The initial Franchise Fee is not refundable and is fully earned by XYZ upon the execution of your Franchise Agreement. The only exception to this is if you fail to complete XYZ's training program to satisfaction. In that event $ _____ will be refunded to you.

NOTE 2: This is an estimate of the monthly rent for a _____ square foot facility in a _____ Building located in an upscale suburban area with easy access to major interstates, Pogo Sticks stores and hotels. The competitive costs of lease space in your area may differ considerably and is dependent upon many variables. We recommend you contact a real estate broker in your area to determine a more accurate estimate.

NOTE 3: This is an estimate of the total cost. The items considered in the estimate are _____. All of the above items are required to be purchased in accordance with our specifications and instructions. Because this equipment and the related installation services can be obtained from a wide range of vendors and suppliers it is difficult to predict the exact cost. We recommend you obtain estimates from a variety of companies before making your choice since pricing in these areas is very competitive. While we do specify the type and brand of equipment to be utilized, we do not require you to purchase from a designated source or supplier.

NOTE 4: This is an estimate of your initial working capital needs for the first six (6) months. Actual needs may vary. This is an important item, however, and we recommend you overestimate your needs rather than underestimate.

NOTE 5: XYZ relied on a number of years of experience in the Pogo Sticks store business to compile these estimates. You should review the figures carefully with a business advisor before making a decision to purchase the franchise.

ITEM 8
RESTRICTIONS ON SOURCES
OF PRODUCTS AND SERVICES

You must purchase from XYZ or its designated supplier promotional items specified by XYZ. XYZ must make such promotional items available to you at cost, plus administrative costs incurred by XYZ in providing promotional items to you. XYZ has the sole discretion to determine what promotional items are required and who are designated suppliers. Promotional items include _____, _____, _____, sign stand, hats, and shirts. XYZ negotiates purchase arrangements with suppliers, including price terms, for your benefit. XYZ does not derive any income from the sale of these items. XYZ does not provide material benefits to you (for example renewal or granting additional franchises) based on your use of designated or approved services. The promotional items you are required to buy constitute approximately $_____ or less than _____ % of all purchases required by you to open a Pogo Sticks store.

Except as stated above, you are not required to purchase or lease any goods, services, supplies, fixtures, equipment, or inventory relating to the establishment or operation of the Pogo Sticks store business from XYZ or from any sources designated by XYZ.

XYZ does not require you to purchase from it supplies, fixtures, equipment, inventory, or other materials required to be used in the operation of a XYZ Pogo Sticks store.

You are required to purchase supplies and materials required for a XYZ Pogo Sticks store in accordance with specifications provided by XYZ from suppliers approved (and not thereafter disapproved) by XYZ. XYZ's product specifications are set forth in its Planning Design Standards Manual. The specifications may include standards as to strength, finish, and appearance. You may purchase all supplies and materials meeting these specifications from XYZ or approved suppliers. XYZ may establish additional specifications and written notice will be sent to you. XYZ may issue and alter specifications for those items by changes in or additions to the Confidential Operating Manual by giving written notice to you.

If you propose to purchase or lease supplies, products, or other items from suppliers that have not been approved by XYZ, you will be required to give XYZ a written request for approval of such supplier on the form provided for that purpose in the Confidential Operating Manual (the Deviation Request form). You must not enter into any purchase agreement with a supplier until that supplier has been approved by XYZ. You will be required to submit specifications, drawings, photographs, samples, and other relevant information for examination and/or testing by XYZ. XYZ will notify you of its decision to approve or reject the supplier within 30 days of the receipt of your request for approval (provided all required information and testing has been completed). You must not sell or dispense any products or activities except those specifically recognized and approved by XYZ as part of your business. XYZ maintains a list of approved suppliers at its corporate office.

Neither XYZ nor persons affiliated with XYZ derive revenue as a result of required purchases or leases by you in accordance with specifications or standards prescribed by XYZ, or from suppliers approved by XYZ. There are no goods or services required in the operation of the Pogo Sticks store for which XYZ or persons affiliated with XYZ are the only approved suppliers.

ITEM 9
FRANCHISEE'S OBLIGATIONS

THIS TABLE LISTS YOUR PRINCIPAL OBLIGATIONS UNDER THE FRANCHISE AND OTHER AGREEMENTS. IT WILL HELP YOU FIND MORE DETAILED INFORMATION ABOUT YOUR OBLIGATIONS IN THESE AGREEMENTS AND IN OTHER ITEMS OF THIS OFFERING CIRCULAR.

Obligation	Section In Agreement	Item In Offering Circular

(Schedule deleted)

ITEM 10
FINANCING

XYZ does not offer, either directly or indirectly, any financing arrangements. XYZ does not guarantee your note, lease, or obligation.

ITEM 11
FRANCHISOR'S OBLIGATIONS

Except as listed below, XYZ need not provide any assistance to you. Before you open your business, XYZ will:

1. If you are interested in developing multiple locations, identify a Territory with you, and create a Development Schedule. (Development Agreement—Sections _____ and _____.)
2. If you are opening a single location, accept a geographic area for the location of the Pogo Sticks store. (Franchise Agreement—Section _____ and _____.)
3. Assist in selecting a location upon which the Pogo Sticks store will be developed. (Franchise Agreement—Section _____.) Generally, XYZ does not own the premises where the Pogo Sticks stores are located.
4. Provide XYZ's standards and specifications for the development of the Pogo Sticks store, including all equipment necessary thereto, and a list of the supplies and products which must be purchased prior to the commencement of the Pogo Sticks store operation. (Franchise Agreement—Section _____.)
5. Review your signage, construction plans, and Pogo Sticks store floor plans for compliance with the Planning Design Standards Manual. (Franchise Agreement—Section _____.)

6. After approving you as a qualified applicant for a Franchise and after the execution of the Development and Franchise Agreements by you, and before opening the Pogo Sticks store, XYZ will train your principal owner(s) and management staff through their attendance at XYZ's Initial Training Program. The Initial Training Program for your principal owner(s) and management staff is conducted for a minimum of _____ weeks and, if XYZ requires, up to _____ weeks if XYZ feels the principal owner(s) or management staff requires such additional training. XYZ's Initial Training Program is outlined in Exhibit _____. (Franchise Agreement—Section _____.)

7. For a period before opening and after opening the Pogo Sticks store (the length of time as determined by XYZ) provide one or more of XYZ's representatives for the purpose of facilitating the opening of the Pogo Sticks store. You must pay all room, board, and travel expenses of XYZ's representatives, reasonably incurred. (Franchise Agreement—Section _____.)

8. Provide promotional materials and bulletins on new sales techniques, marketing developments, products, and operational systems, when available. (Franchise Agreement—Section _____.)

9. Loan to you one set of all of XYZ's Manuals, containing mandatory and suggested specifications, standards, operating procedures, and rules prescribed by XYZ, as well as information relative to your other obligations under the Franchise Agreement and the operation of the Pogo Sticks store. All Manuals will remain confidential and the property of XYZ. (Franchise Agreement—Section _____.)

XYZ, although not obligated to do so by the Franchise Agreement or any other agreement, may:

10. Provide additional training programs, at your expense, as reasonably requested by you during the term of the Franchise Agreement. (Franchise Agreement—Section _____.)
11. Provide promotional materials and bulletins on new sales techniques, marketing developments, products, and operational systems which may be developed by XYZ. (Franchise Agreement—Section _____.)

During the operation of your business, XYZ will:

1. At XYZ's expense, visit your location for the purpose of evaluating your compliance with the Franchise Agreement and the XYZ Operating System. (Franchise Agreement—Section _____.)
2. If you enter into Cooperative Advertising Programs with other Franchisees and/or XYZ, provide guidance and assistance. (Franchise Agreement—Section _____.)
3. Develop, through XYZ's Production Fund, certain marketing materials and programs, as XYZ determines. (Franchise Agreement—Section _____.)

XYZ is not obligated to do so by the Franchise Agreement or any other agreement, but may:

4. Provide information regarding new products and engage in the development of new product methods for Pogo Sticks store operations. (Franchise Agreement—Section _____.)
5. Provide, at your expense, additional assistance and training as reasonably requested by you during the operation of the Pogo Sticks store. (Franchise Agreement—Section _____.)
6. Provide new sales techniques, marketing developments, products, and operational systems. (Franchise Agreement—Section _____.)

7. Protect and defend, at XYZ's sole election, XYZ's marks, service marks, and other proprietary property. (Franchise Agreement—Section _____.)

8. Establish and maintain a national advertising fund to promote and advertise the XYZ Franchise System generally. (Franchise Agreement—Section _____.)

Advertising is done in a wide variety of media, including television, radio, newspaper, and flyers. In regard to advertising:

1. Local Advertising—You must spend at least _____% of your monthly gross sales on local advertising and promotion. Advertising expenditures must be made directly by you, subject to XYZ's or XYZ's designated advertising agency's approval and direction. By the 25th of each month you must provide XYZ with a Marketing Report, as defined in the Franchise Agreement. (Franchise Agreement—Section _____.) In addition, from the time you execute the Franchise Agreement until one month following the actual opening of the Pogo Sticks store, you must spend an additional amount, as determined by XYZ, on local advertising promotion. (Franchise Agreement—Section _____.)

2. Cooperative Advertising—If XYZ determines that two or more XYZ Pogo Sticks stores are located in close proximity so as to result in a Common Marketing Area, as defined in the Franchise Agreement, upon request from XYZ, you must participate in a Cooperative Agreement to engage the services of an advertising agency to cooperate with XYZ to administer, place and schedule a joint advertising program. XYZ has the sole power to require a Cooperative Agreement between Pogo Sticks stores to be formed, changed, dissolved,

or merged. Cooperative Agreements are governed by a Cooperative Advertising Group Agreement, which is available for your review upon your reasonable request. Under the Cooperative Agreement, you must expend at least _____% of your Pogo Sticks store's gross sales. Each Cooperative must report its advertising expenditures on a monthly basis in accordance with the Marketing Report's requirements and within 60 days after the end of each calendar year. Contributions made under a Cooperative Agreement are credited toward monthly Local Advertising expenditure requirements. (Franchise Agreement—Section _____.) XYZ, an officer elected by the members of the Cooperative, and an independent Certified Public Accountant administer the Cooperative. The Cooperative prepares periodic monthly financial statements which are available for your review upon your reasonable request.

3. National Fund (if established)—In addition to local and cooperative advertising requirements, you must pay weekly, at the time royalties are paid, an amount not to exceed _____% of the gross sales of the Pogo Sticks store to the national advertising fund ("National Fund"), when established. The contribution amount may be set by XYZ at the time the National Fund is established and may be changed at any time so long as it does not exceed ___% of gross sales. None of your contributions are refundable. XYZ may not be able to require all franchisees to participate in the National Fund due to the fact that many existing franchise agreements do not impose a requirement to participate in the National Fund upon franchisees; however, unless prevented by the terms of an existing agreement, XYZ will require all new franchisees and renewing franchisees to participate in the National Fund. It is anticipated that the National Fund,

when established, will be used to produce and disseminate television advertisements that will be shown nationally or in certain regional areas. In addition, it is anticipated that internationally-based franchisees will contribute to the National Fund and that a portion of the Fund will be devoted to international advertising—most likely in specific international markets where franchisees are located. XYZ will use a combination of its in-house advertising department and a national or regional advertising agency to produce and disseminate this type of national/regional advertising. All franchisees (whose agreements provide for contribution to the National Fund) must contribute to the National Fund. XYZ (or any company-owned Pogo Sticks stores, if any are established) is not required to contribute to the National Fund, although it is anticipated that voluntary contributions will be made. XYZ will administer the National Fund, audit it on an annual basis and make the financial statements available to you upon request. XYZ may receive payment for providing certain in-house advertising department services. XYZ is not required to spend any specific amount from the National Fund on advertising in the area where your franchise is located. If all fees contributed to the National Fund are not spent in the year in which they are collected, XYZ will carry all funds forward for use in future years. No portion of the National Fund is used for advertising that is principally a solicitation for the sale of franchises. (Franchise Agreement—Section _____.)

4. Production Fund—In addition to local, cooperative and national advertising requirements, you must pay weekly, at the time royalties are paid, an amount equal to ___% of the gross sales of the Pogo Sticks store to XYZ's Production Fund. XYZ's company-owned Pogo Sticks stores (if any)

must also contribute an amount equal to ___% of the gross sales of the Pogo Sticks store to XYZ Production Fund. XYZ and an independent certified public accountant administer the Production Fund. The Production Fund is audited and financial statements of the Production Fund are available for review upon your reasonable request. XYZ's employees who perform services for the Production Fund receive part of their compensation from this fund. XYZ has the sole discretion to determine this fund's expenditures towards furtherance of advertising programs. For the past fiscal year, the total expenses paid, in percentages, by the Production Fund is as follows: administrative services and casual labor: ___%; promotions: ___%; professional fees: ___%; print production: ___%; printing expense: ___%; and other expenses (including, but not limited to, office and art supplies, postage/shipping, incentives, electronic production, travel expenses, consulting fees, and prizes): ___%. (Franchise Agreement—Section _____.)

As part of your local advertising requirement, you must maintain a business phone and advertise continuously in the classified and Yellow Pages of the local telephone directory under the listing "Pogo Sticks stores" using mats approved in advance by XYZ. (Franchise Agreement—Section _____.) You must use all trademarks and service marks required by XYZ. (Franchise Agreement— Section _____.)

For all of the above advertising requirements, you must submit the advertisement or promotional material to XYZ or its designated agency for its prior approval. (Franchise Agreement—Section _____.)

In regard to computer hardware and cash registers to be used by you at your Pogo Sticks store, XYZ requires you to obtain a

Point of Sale System to process Pogo Sticks store orders. XYZ does not require you to obtain any specific Point of Sale system. However, XYZ recommends that you obtain the _____ or any equivalent system. The _____ can be purchased directly from _____, [telephone number] , or through XYZ.

Your Point of Sale System must process all Pogo Sticks store orders, track employee hours and payroll, and print customer receipts. In addition, your Point of Sale System or another separate system must be able to perform credit card processing. XYZ will not have independent access to the information and data contained on your Point of Sale System. The size of the Pogo Sticks store dictates how many terminals your Point of Sale System will need. The standard configuration for a _____ square foot Pogo Sticks store is _____ terminals.

Under this standard configuration, as of _____ [date], the Sales Computer sells for $_____, but, if you purchase the Sales Computer through XYZ, you will receive a _____% discount and, as a result, it is currently costing $_____ under this means of purchasing. You have an obligation to upgrade or update your Point of Sale System as XYZ may require. (Section _____ of the Franchise Agreement.) It is also recommended that you obtain an office computer with characteristics equivalent to or greater than: _____ RAM; _____ MB Hard Drive; Color Monitor; _____ Floppy Drive and MS-DOS 6.2. If you choose not to use the _____, with its attached printer, then you are required to obtain an office printer of comparable or greater quality than the _____ Printer. (Section _____ of the Franchise Agreement.) You are not required to purchase any computer software. However, it is recommended that you obtain _____, which is a spreadsheet program. If you desire to use XYZ's inventory system, which you are not required to do, you must use the _____ program to access this information. As of _____, 19—, the

_____ program costs $_____. It is also recommended that you obtain a word processing program such as Professional Write, Word Perfect, or other comparable program to assist in office word processing. XYZ will assist you in obtaining the above-referenced computer hardware, cash registers, and software.

In regard to location of your Pogo Sticks store, it is your responsibility to select the location of your Pogo Sticks store within its designated area. Your location must be acceptable to XYZ. Criteria considered by XYZ in the location-approval process will vary, but typically includes a neighboring population density of at least 10,000 persons per Pogo Sticks store, traffic patterns, adequate parking, type of building the Pogo Sticks store will be located in, proximity to shopping malls, other commercial and office buildings, other XYZ Pogo Sticks stores, and other similar type Pogo Sticks stores in the area. XYZ will approve or disapprove your proposed location within 60 days. (Franchise Agreement—Section _____.)

The usual length of time between the execution of the Franchise Agreement by you, and the opening of the Pogo Sticks store for business is ___ to ___ days. Factors affecting such length of time usually include obtaining a satisfactory site, financing arrangements, meeting local ordinances or community requirements, delivery and installation of equipment and signs, obtaining a license, and other factors. (Franchise Agreement—Section _____.)

Before opening, XYZ offers an Initial Training Program instructing your principal owner(s) and management staff in the day-to-day operation of the Pogo Sticks store. Attendance is mandatory for your principal owner and management staff. The Initial Training Program is conducted in _____, for a minimum period of _____ weeks and, if XYZ requires, up to _____ weeks. The training program is conducted before the opening of the Pogo Sticks store for business. The training program shall cover all aspects of the operation of an XYZ Franchise, including the XYZ Operating System, financial controls, marketing techniques, service techniques, deployment of labor, advertising methods, and instruction on maintaining professional standards.

After the opening of the Pogo Sticks store, XYZ, in its sole discretion, may require your management staff to take additional retraining. Such retraining may occur at your Pogo Sticks store or such other locations as XYZ, in its sole discretion, determines. The length and duration of the retraining program is determined by XYZ. If retraining occurs within six months following the opening of the Pogo Sticks store, you must pay all reasonable expenses incurred by XYZ's employees for travel and lodging, but you are not required to reimburse XYZ's employees' salaries. If retraining occurs after the Pogo Sticks store has been in operation for six months, you must reimburse XYZ's employees for the reasonable cost of travel, lodging, and salaries. You must reimburse each member of XYZ's retraining team at the rate of $_____ per day if such retraining occurs at your Pogo Sticks store, and at the rate of $_____ per day if such retraining occurs at a site selected by XYZ.

There is no tuition charged for you or your employees for attending the Initial Training Program, however, you are responsible for the payment of all expenses associated with your training and the training offered to your employees, which includes lodging, food, travel, and employee compensation. XYZ reserves the right to disapprove any participant as having successfully completed the Initial Training Program. The Initial Training Program is more specifically described in Exhibit _____. The instructors for the Initial Training Program are _____. XYZ may offer in its sole discretion future refresher training programs for previously trained and experienced franchisees at a location to be designated by XYZ. There is no charge by XYZ for these courses. You are responsible for the payment of all expenses associated with such additional training which includes lodging, food, travel, and employee compensation. (Franchise Agreement—Section _____.)

ITEM 12
TERRITORY

XYZ will, under the Development Agreement, reserve for you an agreed-upon number of XYZ Pogo Sticks stores within the Territory in accordance with the Development Schedule.

During the term of the Development Agreement, XYZ may not grant to any other party the right to develop, construct, own, or operate an XYZ Pogo Sticks store in the Territory and may not establish company-owned XYZ Pogo Sticks stores therein.

XYZ may, however, use and franchise within the Territory any other trade names and trademarks that it might develop and not include in the Operating System, as that term is defined in the Development Agreement and the Franchise Agreement, for use with similar or different franchise systems for the sale of other products or services.

In the Franchise Agreement for a single location, you are given the individual right to use the XYZ Operating System at your Pogo Sticks store location within a specific geographic location ("Franchise Area"). No other XYZ Pogo Sticks store may be established or operated within the Franchise Area as delineated and defined in Section _____ of the Franchise Agreement. The Franchise Area may not by altered without your approval. Unless stated in the Development Agreement, you do not have any rights of first refusal or similar rights to acquire additional franchises within the Franchise Area or contiguous areas.

In Section _____ of the Franchise Agreement, XYZ reserves the right to issue and franchise within the Franchise Area any of the trademarks, service marks, or other proprietary property rights that it may develop and not designate as rights granted in the Franchise Agreement, for use with similar or different franchise systems for the sale of the same, similar, or different products or services other than in connection with the XYZ Pogo Sticks store. In addition, XYZ may develop, merchandise, sell, and license others to sell XYZ related products to the public, to non-Pogo Sticks store outlets in the Franchise Area.

XYZ has not reserved and may not reserve any right to franchise or establish company-owned outlets under a different service mark or tradename that may be engaged in the same or similar lines of service as those being offered by you within your trading or marketing area.

As of the date of this Offering Circular, XYZ has not formulated plans or policies to operate or franchise the operation of any business selling services or products under different trade names, service marks, or trademark goods, similar to or competitive with those to be offered for sale by the franchise contemplated herein.

There are no restrictions contained in the Franchise Agreement which prohibit you, other franchisees, or XYZ from soliciting sales or accepting business from outside their franchise areas.

The continuation of your right to operate an XYZ Pogo Sticks store in the Franchise Area is not dependent upon the achievement of a specified sales volume, market penetration, or other contingency.

ITEM 13
TRADEMARKS

A reproduction of the primary service marks appears on the cover sheet of this Offering Circular. Service marks, trademarks, and commercial symbols (sometimes hereinafter collectively referred to as the "Marks") may be created and designated by XYZ for use in the future in connection with new advertising campaigns or business formats. All right, title, and interest in the Marks is held and will be held by XYZ. In the Franchise Agreement, XYZ grants to you the right to use and operate a XYZ Pogo Sticks store under the trade names "XYZ ," "_____ ," and "_____". XYZ may change or modify its Marks, and you are obligated to adopt, use, and display the new or modified trade names, service marks, trademarks, and copyrighted materials at your expense.

XYZ has been granted registrations on the Principal Federal Register for the following service marks:

1. Registration No. _____, registered _____, International Class _____, for Pogo Sticks store services.
2. Registration No. _____, registered _____, International Class _____, for Pogo Sticks store services.
3. Registration No. _____, registered _____, International Class _____, for Pogo Sticks store services.

There are no presently effective determinations of the United States Patent and Trademark Office, the Trademark Administrator of any State, or of any Court and no pending interference, opposition, or cancellation proceeding or pending material litigation involving the trademarks, service marks, tradenames, logotypes, or other commercial symbols of XYZ.

There are no agreements currently in effect that significantly limit the rights of XYZ to use or license the use of its trademarks, service marks, tradenames, logotypes, or other commercial symbols in any manner material to the XYZ Franchises being offered here.

XYZ, as a matter of current practice, is taking prudent steps to protect your rights to use the "XYZ" service marks, trade names, logotypes, and other commercial symbols by applying for Federal and State trademark and service mark registrations and Corporate Name registrations where XYZ deems appropriate. While XYZ has no obligation under the Franchise Agreement to take these steps, it is its present intent to obtain registrations whenever practicable. According to the Franchise Agreement, you must notify XYZ if you learn of any person, firm, or organization using the name "XYZ" or a substantially similar name, or using trademarks, service marks, or methods of procedures which may constitute an infringement upon the trade names, service marks, trademarks, copyrights, or trade secrets of XYZ. Further, according to the terms of the Franchise Agreement, you agree to promptly notify XYZ of all claims, demands, or suits based upon any attempt by any party to use the XYZ Marks. You must cooperate with and assist XYZ regarding the protection of the XYZ Marks and XYZ Operating System and other products and items delivered to you. XYZ, in its sole discretion, may elect to commence a defense or prosecution of any litigation arising out of the Marks, whether instituted by any person, firm, corporation, or governmental agency against XYZ or you. Although XYZ does not believe the following information materially affects your use of our Marks, XYZ has discovered that _____ is currently operating a Pogo Sticks store, featuring _____ and _____, in the state of _____ under the name 'XYZ' registered 'XYZ' in the state of _____ on _____ and claims a date of first use in January 1972. XYZ believes its rights to the use of the name 'XYZ' are superior and separately registered the Marks in the state of _____ in June of 1995.

There are no infringing uses known to XYZ which materially affect your use of the trademarks, service marks, trade names, logotypes, or other commercial symbols.

ITEM 14
PATENTS, COPYRIGHTS
AND PROPRIETARY INFORMATION

XYZ has no rights on any patent. XYZ has filed for patent protection on its Super-Duper Pro K Model pogo stick, Application No. _____, filed on _____, but no patent has been granted as of the date of this circular. XYZ claims common law copyrights on its materials, including the XYZ manuals, charts, films, tapes, and printed materials. There are no agreements currently in effect that significantly limit the rights of XYZ to use or license the use of the copyrights in any manner material to you.

ITEM 15
OBLIGATION TO PARTICIPATE
IN THE ACTUAL OPERATION
OF THE FRANCHISE BUSINESS

According to the Franchise Agreement, either you or an approved manager is required to participate personally in the daily on-premises supervision of the XYZ Pogo Sticks store. You or an approved manager must attend and successfully complete XYZ's Initial Training Program, as quickly as is possible based on the scheduling of the training program and be approved by XYZ.

approved by XYZ. Upon the death, disability, or termination of the employment of an approved manager, you are required to appoint a new approved manager within 30 days. The successor approved manager must attend and successfully complete the Initial Training Program and be approved by XYZ.

ITEM 16
RESTRICTIONS ON WHAT
FRANCHISEE MAY SELL

In order to establish and maintain uniform standards, quality and appearance, you agree to sell or offer for sale to the public only articles, products, and services as approved by XYZ. You agree not to sell or offer any products or services not authorized by XYZ and agree not to use the Franchise premises for any purpose other than the operation of the Pogo Sticks store.

You are required by the Franchise Agreement to utilize the licensed rights (including trademarks, trade names, service marks, and logos) only in connection with the Franchise business.

ITEM 17
RENEWAL, TERMINATION, TRANSFER
AND DISPUTE RESOLUTION

This table lists important provisions of the franchise and related Agreements. You should read these provisions in the Agreements attached to this Offering Circular.

Provision	Secion in Franchise Agreement	Summary

(Schedule deleted)

These states have statutes which may supersede the Franchise Agreement in your relationship with XYZ International including the areas of termination and renewal of your franchise: ARKANSAS [Stat. Section 70-807]; CALIFORNIA [Bus. & Prof. Code Sections 20000-20043]; CONNECTICUT [Gen. Stat. Section 42-133e et seq.]; DELAWARE [Code, tit.]; HAWAII [Rev. Stat. Section 482E-1]; ILLINOIS [815 ILCS 705/19 and 705/20]; INDIANA [Stat. Section 23-2-2.7]; IOWA [Code Sections 523H.1-523H.17]; MICHIGAN [Stat. Section 19.854(27)]; MINNESOTA [Stat. Section 80C.14]; MISSISSIPPI [Code Section 75-24-51]; MISSOURI [Stat. Section 407.400]; NEBRASKA (Rev. Stat. Section 87-401]; NEW JERSEY [Stat. Section 56: 10-1]; SOUTH DAKOTA [Codified Laws Section 37-5A-51]; VIRGINIA [Code 13.1-557-574-13.1-564]; WASHINGTON [Code Section 19.100.180]; WISCONSIN [Stat. Section 135.03]. These and other states may have court decisions which may supersede the Franchise Agreement in your relationship with XYZ International including the areas of termination and renewal of your franchise. For additional information, please see Exhibit _____ attached to this Offering Circular.

The Franchise Agreement provides for termination upon bankruptcy. This provision may not be enforceable under federal bankruptcy law (11 U.S.C.A. Sec. 101 et seq.).

ITEM 18
PUBLIC FIGURES

XYZ does not use any public figures to promote its Franchises.

ITEM 19
EARNINGS CLAIMS

XYZ provides, as part of this Offering Circular, information regarding the earnings capability of XYZ's Franchisees. This information is attached as Exhibit _____. While this information is provided to assist in the analysis of an XYZ Franchise, YOU ARE ADVISED THAT EACH NEW FRANCHISEE'S INDIVIDUAL FINANCIAL RESULTS ARE LIKELY TO BE DIFFERENT FROM THE RESULTS STATED IN EXHIBIT _____. THE INFORMATION SUPPLIED IS BASED UPON AVERAGES OF XYZ'S FRANCHISES.

Upon your request, XYZ will make available to you the substantiating data used in preparing the averages of earnings capability presented in Exhibit _____.

ITEM 20
LIST OF OUTLETS

Information concerning our franchisees and other outlets appears in the following tables. In addition, the names, addresses and telephone numbers of XYZ International's franchisees are contained in Exhibit _____ of this Offering Circular.

(Schedule deleted)

ITEM 21
FINANCIAL STATEMENTS

Attached as Exhibit _____ are audited financial statements for the fiscal years _____, _____, and _____.

ITEM 22
CONTRACTS

Copies of the Development Agreement and Franchise Agreement to be used by XYZ in this State are attached hereto as Exhibits _____ and _____ respectively.

ITEM 23
RECEIPT

Attached as Exhibit _____ of this Offering Circular is a receipt to be signed by you.

B

SAMPLE FRANCHISE
AGREEMENT

XYZ
FRANCHISE AGREEMENT

DATE: _____
PARTIES: [Name of Franchisor],
    a[n] _____ [state of incorporation]
    corporation   (Franchisor)
      Address:
    [Franchisor's Address]
    [Name of Franchisee]   (Franchisee)
    Address:
    [Franchisee's Address]

RECITALS:

A. Franchisor is the owner of the name and trademark "_____"
and related logo types and is the owner of a system to offer
franchise businesses to [description of franchise business].
B. The Franchise program, includes but is not limited to: common use and promotion of the name _____ .

C. Franchisee warrants and represents that the Franchisee is familiar with Franchisor and its operation, has reviewed the Offering Circular provided by Franchisor, and has been provided with such other information concerning the operation of a franchise as Franchisee requested.

D. Franchisee warrants and represents that the Franchisee does not wish to obtain the franchise for speculative or investment purposes and has no present intention to sell or transfer or attempt to sell or transfer said franchise in whole or in part. Franchisee understands and acknowledges the importance of the high and uniform standards of quality, appearance, and service imposed by Franchisor in order to maintain the value of Franchisor's name and the necessity of operating the franchise in compliance with Franchisor's standards.

AGREEMENTS:

SECTION 1. FRANCHISE

1.1 Grant of Franchise. Franchisor hereby grants to Franchisee the exclusive right and license to operate a _____ business for a term of five years from the date of this Agreement in Franchisee's exclusive area and to use the Franchisor's method of advertising, trade name, logos, and the rights enumerated herein solely in a _____ business and in no other manner.

1.2 Franchisee's Area. Franchisee acknowledges that Franchisor's method is designed to operate on the basis that each Franchisee is assigned a specific exclusive geographical area in which each Franchisee must use its best efforts to develop and service in accordance with Franchisor's standards and specifications. Therefore, the license granted herein is specifically limited to the right to operate the _____ business within the Franchisee's Area, more fully set forth in Section 21.2 of this Agreement.

SECTION 2. INITIAL FRANCHISE FEE AND TERM

2.1 Initial Franchise Fee. The Franchisee shall pay to Franchisor an initial franchise fee, payable concurrently with the execution of this Agreement, of $_____, which fee is fully earned by Franchisor upon the signing of this Agreement and is nonrefundable.

2.2 Term. The term of this Agreement and the right to operate the franchise granted herein shall commence as of the date of acceptance, as indicated herein upon final execution hereof by Franchisor, and shall continue in effect for five years, unless a termination or breach shall occur as provided.

SECTION 3. OTHER FEES AND OTHER CONTINUING CHARGES

3.1 Royalty.

3.1.1 Monthly Royalty. In addition to the initial franchise fee, Franchisee shall pay Franchisor a monthly royalty payment equal to five percent of monthly gross sales from Franchisee's business. Gross sales is defined in Section 3.1.2.

3.1.2 Gross Sales. For the purpose of this Agreement, gross sales shall mean all receipts, whether in cash or on credit: (i) from Franchisee's business; (ii) from all other activities of every type and description done by Franchisee or any person employed by Franchise under the name _____ or in connection with any of its trademarks or service marks; and (iii) from any other related business operated by Franchisee or any person employed by Franchisee whether or not the name and marks of Franchisor are used.

3.1.3 Payment. The monthly royalty payments shall be due and payable without invoice or other notice from Franchisor on the 15th day of the month following the month for which payment is due, upon the form prescribed by Franchisor.

3.1.4 Late Charge and Costs. If royalty payments are not fully paid on or before the date when due, Franchisee agrees to pay Franchisor a late charge equal to two percent per month on all amounts due and unpaid. In addition, Franchisee agrees to reimburse Franchisor for all costs of collection, including attorney's fees, of any amounts due under this Agreement.

3.2 Advertising. Franchisee shall pay Franchisor a monthly advertising fee equal to one percent of monthly gross sales (as defined in Section 3.1.2) from Franchisee's business. This amount shall be due and payable without invoice or other notice from Franchisor on the 15th day of the month following the month for which payment is due, upon the form prescribed by Franchisor. Payment shall be made separately from other payments to Franchisor and shall be paid to "Ad-Fund." Franchisor shall place all advertising fees received from Franchisees in a segregated advertising fund, the proceeds of which shall be expended solely upon advertising for Franchisees, subject to reasonable administrative fees and costs charged by Franchisor. The advertising fee and fund are more fully described in Section 7.3 of this Agreement.

SECTION 4. NATURE AND VALUE
OF FRANCHISE NAME, TRADEMARKS,
TRADE SECRETS, AND GOOD WILL

4.1 Authorized Use. The franchise granted hereby authorizes the Franchisee to use Franchisor's trademarks, know-how, and trade secrets in the operation of a business as set forth in this Agreement.

4.2 No Transfer. Nothing contained in this Agreement or done pursuant to this Agreement shall be deemed to give the Franchisee any right or interest in any of the trademarks, trade secrets, and know-how of Franchisor. Franchisee agrees further, having under this Agreement received secrets, know-how, experience, and assistance, now and hereafter provided by Franchisor, for the purpose of establishment and operation of a _____ business and having been granted participation in the commercial benefits of the good will provided by Franchisor, that Franchisee will not at any time divulge any secret or confidential information concerning the business of Franchisor and that upon termination or transfer of Franchisee's franchise, Franchisee will not at any time thereafter in any manner use, copy, or imitate any of the trademarks of Franchisor or trade upon Franchisor's good will. The Franchisee further agrees that in the event of a violation of any of Franchisee's obligations under this Section 4.2, Franchisor may immediately obtain an injunction from a court of competent jurisdiction without any requirement of bond, in addition to any other remedies.

4.3 Benefit. Any use of the Franchisor's trademarks by a Franchisee shall inure to the benefit of Franchisor.

4.4 Limitations on Use. The Franchisee agrees that the trademarks, secrets, and know-how of Franchisor may be used only for the purpose of operating a _____ business in the agreed territory and shall not be used by Franchisee for any purpose or in any manner not authorized by Franchisor and that, at all times during the entire term of this agreement, the Franchisee will diligently and loyally use the Franchisee's best efforts to promote such business and to enhance the good will of, and customer demand for, the franchise business.

4.5 Name. The trademarks, including without limitation, the mark _____ or any variation thereof, shall not be used as a part of the firm or corporate name of the Franchisee but shall be distinguished and set apart from the firm or corporate name of any Franchisee.

4.6 Other Goods or Services. In no way are any of Franchisor's trademarks or trade name to be used or misrepresented as names or marks for the sale of any goods or services not specified in this Agreement.

4.7 State Registration. Franchisee shall take steps to register, if not previously registered, the trademark of _____ with the state in which said Franchisee is located. Said registration shall be in the name of Franchisor and shall be at the Franchisee's expense. Franchisee shall notify Franchisor of the registration and shall provide all documentation of same to Franchisor.

4.8 Infringement. In the event of any infringement of, or challenge of the Franchisee's use of any name or mark, the Franchisee shall immediately notify Franchisor, and Franchisor will have sole discretion to take such action as it deems appropriate. While Franchisor is not required to defend the Franchisee against any infringement, unfair competition, or other claim respecting the Franchisee's use of any name or mark, Franchisor is obligated to indemnify the Franchisee against, and to reimburse the Franchisee for, all damages for which Franchisee is found liable in any proceeding arising out of the use of any name or mark and for all costs reasonably incurred by the Franchisee in the defense of any such claim, provided that the Franchisee has notified Franchisor of such claim as described above and provided Franchisee made an effort to register the trademark _____ as provided in Section 4.7. The Franchisee agrees not to contest, directly or indirectly, Franchisor's ownership, title, right, or interest in its names or marks, trade secrets, methods, procedures, and advertising techniques which are part of the franchise business or contest Franchisor's sole right to register, use, or license others to use such names and marks, trade secrets, methods, procedures, and techniques.

SECTION 5. RELATIONSHIP OF THE PARTIES

5.1 Independent Contractor. The nature of the relationship between Franchisee and Franchisor is and shall be an independent contractor and nothing herein contained shall be construed so as to create an agency relationship, a partnership or joint venture between Franchisor and Franchisee. Neither Franchisor nor the Franchisee shall act as agent for the other and neither the Franchisee nor Franchisor shall guarantee the obligations of the other or in any way become obligated for the debts or expenses of the other unless agreed to in writing.

5.2 Operation of Franchisee's Business. Franchisor shall not regulate the hiring or firing of Franchisee's employees. The conduct of the Franchisee's business and employees and the solicitation of customers by Franchisee and Franchisee's employees shall be determined in its own judgment and discretion, subject only to the Policy and Procedures Manual as it may be adopted or revised from time to time by Franchisor.

SECTION 6. OBLIGATIONS OF FRANCHISOR

Franchisor agrees, in consideration of Franchisee's promises contained in this Agreement, to assist Franchisee in providing the Franchisee with the following services:

6.1 Training Program. Franchisor will operate a one (1) week training program for the Franchisee at _____ or any other location that Franchisor may later choose. The training program will consist of Franchisor's operational procedures, marketing system, operation, basic bookkeeping, and accounting, and all aspects of general operations. No additional fee is charged for training. However, Franchisee shall be responsible for all travel, lodging, and sustenance expenses for Franchisee or any employee.

6.2 Promotional or Merchandising Methods. Franchisor may from time to time offer Franchisee suggested promotional or merchandising methods. Any such promotion or merchandising methods will be offered at the discretion of Franchisor according to the currently approved Policy and Procedures Manual of Franchisor.

6.3 Consultation and Advice. Franchisor shall provide ongoing consultation and advice to Franchisee.

6.4 Continuing Assistance. Franchisor may, in its discretion, provide continuing assistance to Franchisee in such areas set forth in the training program or which may arise from time to time. Franchisor may conduct quarterly sales and franchise consultation meetings at _____. (Attendance by Franchisee is voluntary.)

6.5 Marketing. Franchisor shall establish Franchisee's exclusive territory and shall assist Franchisee with the identification of and analysis of the initial targeted minimum households required to begin the operation of Franchisee's business. Franchisor shall also assist Franchisee with the purchase of the necessary mailing lists and other components necessary to the operation of the business.

6.6 Initial Supplies. Franchisor shall supply and provide Franchisee's initial supply of [describe goods provided]. After the initial supply, Franchisee shall pay the prices then in effect for said items to Franchisor. Franchisor will derive income from the sale of these items to Franchisee.

6.7 Policy and Procedures Manual. Franchisor shall develop and provide a Policy and Procedures Manual for the management and operation of Franchisee's business which may be updated from time to time.

6.8 Advertising. Franchisor may assist, but is not required to assist, Franchisee in obtaining national or regional advertising accounts and coordinate the placement of said advertisements among and between all Franchisees who desire to accept or secure said advertisers or advertisements in accordance with this Agreement.

SECTION 7. OBLIGATIONS OF THE FRANCHISEE

Franchisee agrees, in consideration of Franchisor's promises contained in this Agreement, as follows:

7.1 Payments. Franchisee shall pay promptly to Franchisor (or its designated suppliers) any fees due hereunder, as well as charges for any products or services furnished by Franchisor (or its designated suppliers) at Franchisee's request, including but not limited to (i) the initial franchise fee set forth in Section 2.1; (ii) the royalty payments as set forth in Section 3.1; (iii) the advertising fee as set forth in Section 3.2; and (iv) any other charges incurred under this Agreement by Franchisee.

7.2 Reports. Franchisee shall report to Franchisor by the 15th day of the following month, on forms required by Franchisor, the amount of monthly gross sales and royalty payments due for the previous month. In addition, Franchisee shall report to Franchisor, on forms prescribed by Franchisor, the general financial condition of Franchisee's business specifying expenses, costs, income, profit, and so forth on January 30th, April 30th, July 30th and October 30th of each year for the previous quarter of operation prior to each such date.

7.3 Advertising Fund. Franchisee shall contribute one percent of the monthly gross sales from the Franchisee's business to an advertising fund administered and maintained by Franchisor. The fund shall be maintained in a segregated bank account under Franchisor's control, designated as "Ad-Fund." None of the funds are refundable to Franchisee. Franchisor shall use the proceeds of the fund and any interest earned upon said proceeds solely and exclusively for advertising on behalf of Franchisees, subject to reasonable administrative fees and costs charged by Franchisor. Franchisee agrees and acknowledges that Franchisor will administer the fund and the distribution of proceeds for advertising within its absolute discretion. Franchisor reserves the right to apply the proceeds of the fund in whatever manner it deems beneficial to all Franchisees, including an uneven distribution of the proceeds so as to accomplish different goals in different markets. Franchisee acknowledges and agrees that Franchisor may purchase advertising in combination with advertising for its company-owned retail store (if any) and that any such costs for said advertising shall be allocated between Franchisor and the advertising fund on a per store basis for the relevant geographical area. Franchisee shall pay the one percent advertising contribution on the 15th day of the month following the month for which payment is due. Payment shall be due and payable without invoice or other notice from Franchisor and Franchisee is required to report gross sales and the advertising fee due upon the forms prescribed by Franchisor. Payment shall be made separately from other payments to Franchisor and shall be paid to "Ad-Fund."

7.4 Harm to Business. Franchisee shall not engage in any trade, practice, or other activity which is harmful to the good will or reflects unfavorably on the reputation of Franchisor or constitutes deceptive or unfair competition or is in violation of any applicable fair trade law.

7.5 Policy and Procedures Manual. Franchisee shall comply with the Franchisor's Policy and Procedures Manual (if adopted and as it may be revised from time to time) and with all rules and regulations for the good order, uniformity, or protection of the good will and reputation of Franchisor which may from time to time be declared in writing by Franchisor.

7.6 Hold Harmless. Franchisee agrees to hold harmless and protect Franchisor from and against any liability of any kind or nature resulting from the operation of the Franchisee's business. The Franchisee, prior to beginning the operation of Franchisee's business and thereafter, is required to maintain at Franchisee's expense, covering both the Franchisee and Franchisor as named insureds, in a form and with an insurer satisfactory to Franchisor, comprehensive general liability insurance with personal injury coverage of not less than one million dollars ($1,000,000) per occurrence and business interruption insurance in an amount of not less than $100,000 per occurrence. The insurance to be furnished by the Franchisee shall also include motor vehicle insurance with the following coverages and limits: bodily injury liability with limits of $100,000 for any one person and $300,000 for all persons as a result of any one occurrence, property damage liability with limits of $50,000 for any one occurrence, medical payments of $5,000 for each person and uninsured and underinsured coverage, and comprehensive coverage for the actual cash value of each vehicle and $100 deductible collision insurance. Franchisee is also required to maintain worker's compensation insurance, and Franchisor must be a named insured with Franchisee on each insurance policy except worker's compensation insurance. The cost of such insurance and the dates payments are due will vary from one insurer to another. The payments are made directly to the insurer and are ordinarily not refundable.

7.7 Trademarks and Service Marks. Franchisee agrees that from time to time Franchisor may reasonably adopt new or modified trademarks, service marks, or other marks, and Franchisee agrees at Franchisee's expense, to adopt, use, and display for the purposes of this Agreement any such changes as if they were a part of Franchisor's program at the time of the execution of this Agreement.

7.8 Compliance With Law. Franchisee shall comply with all federal, state, and local laws and regulations, and shall obtain, and all times maintain, any and all permits, certificates, or licenses necessary for the full and proper conduct of the business.

7.9 Annual Audit. Franchisee shall conduct an annual audit which, along with the Franchisee's company books, shall be submitted to Franchisor for review within 60 days after December 31 of each year. Said audit shall contain complete and accurate financial statements of Franchisee's business, including a statement of profit and loss and a balance sheet, all prepared in accordance with generally accepted accounting principles.

7.10 Training Program.

7.10.1 Franchisee. Franchisee shall attend a one week training program at Franchisor's headquarters prior to the opening of the franchise.

7.10.2 Others. If the trained Franchisee leaves the franchise business, another person shall take Franchisor's training course so that at least one manager at the franchise business has had the training course. If such other person is required to take the training course, a fee of not more than $1,000 for each additional person taking the course shall be charged Franchisee. The additional training fee shall be due and payable by Franchisee prior to the training session.

7.11 Manager.

7.11.1 Supervision. The franchise business must be at all times under the direct supervision of a Franchisee who has completed the training program.

7.11.2 Identity. Franchisor must be informed of the identity of any manager, whether the Franchisee is an individual, corporation, or partnership, who is at any time utilized or employed by Franchisee.

7.12 Office Equipment. Franchisee shall be required to install and maintain a separate telephone line (or lines), dedicated to the operation of the business, as well as an answering machine for times when the telephone is unable to be answered directly. Territories of 250,000 households or more are required to install and maintain a facsimile machine to communicate with Franchisor and lease or purchase a copy machine. Territories of less than 250,000 households must have access to both facsimile and copying services. All Franchisees shall be required to purchase or lease a portable VHS video playback/monitor and to own or lease a motor vehicle for the purpose of making sales calls, although a specific make or model is not required.

SECTION 8. TERM AND RENEWAL

8.1 Term. The term of the Franchise Agreement is five years from the date of execution of the Franchise Agreement. Additional licenses for territories will be governed by separate Franchise Agreements and with termination dates established therein.

8.2 Commencement of Business. Franchisee is required to commence business operations within one week of the conclusion of Franchisee's training program.

8.3 Option to Renew. Franchisee has an unlimited option to renew the franchise relationship for successive additional five year terms. The Franchisee must give Franchisor at least six months' notice of its intention to exercise its option to renew. Said renewal will be granted if all the conditions of Section 8.4 have been met.

8.4 Conditions of Renewal. The Franchisee will be allowed to renew Franchisee's franchise relationship with Franchisor provided that:

8.4.1 No Breach or Default. The Franchisee is not in breach of any of the terms or conditions of this Agreement and is not in default of any of the provisions of this Agreement requiring payments to be made to Franchisor (or its designated suppliers). Franchisee shall be current on all royalty payments, supply payments, commission payments, and any other fee or payment required hereunder;

8.4.2 Renewal Franchise Agreement. The Franchisee executes a Renewal Franchise Agreement and other legal instruments then customarily used by Franchisor even though the terms, including the amount of royalty fees and other charges, may be materially different from the agreements now in use. Failure or refusal to execute such instruments within 30 days after delivery to the Franchisee shall be deemed an election not to renew the franchise; and

8.4.3 Renewal Fee. The Franchisee pays the renewal fee, not to exceed $1,000.

8.5 Required Notice. If state or local law requires that Franchisor give notice to Franchisee of nonrenewal for noncompliance with this Agreement or the Policy and Procedures Manual prior to the expiration of the term, this Agreement shall remain in effect on a month-to-month basis until Franchisor has given Franchisee the notice required by law.

SECTION 9. TERMINATION

9.1 Termination by Franchisee.

9.1.1 Permitted Termination. If the Franchisee is in compliance with the Franchise Agreement and Franchisor breaches the Agreement and fails to cure such breach within 45 days after written notice of such breach is delivered to Franchisor, the Franchisee may terminate the Franchise Agreement and the franchise, effective 10 days after delivery of written notice to Franchisor of such termination.

9.1.2 Termination in Violation of Agreement. A termination without complying with these requirements or for any reason other than breach of the Franchise Agreement and failure to cure by Franchisor shall be deemed a termination by the Franchisee not in accordance with the provisions of the Franchise Agreement.

9.2 Termination by Franchisor. Franchisor may terminate the Franchise Agreement and the franchise immediately and without other cause, effective 30 days after delivery of notice of termination to the Franchisee, if the Franchisee:

9.2.1 Assignment for Benefit of Creditors. Makes an assignment for the benefit of creditors or an admission of his inability to pay his obligations as they become due;

9.2.2 Bankruptcy or Similar Proceeding. Files a voluntary petition in bankruptcy or any pleading seeking any reorganization, arrangement, composition, adjustment, liquidation, dissolution, or similar relief under any law, or admitting or failing to contest the material allegations of any pleading filed against him, or is adjudicated as bankrupt or insolvent;

9.2.3 Failure to Operate Business. Fails to continuously and actively operate the business;

9.2.4 Inaccurate Statements. Submits two or more statements, one or more annual financial statements, sales or income tax returns, or supporting records to Franchisor that understate by two percent or more the royalties due or materially distort any other material information;

9.2.5 Breach of Payment or Reporting Obligations. Consistently fails to submit when due periodic or annual financial statements or other information or fails to pay when due royalty fees or other fees;

9.2.6 Health and Safety Problems. Violates and fails to cure or consistently violates any health or safety law, ordinance, or regulation or operates the business in a manner that presents a health or safety hazard to its customers or the public;

9.2.7 Unauthorized Assignment. Makes an unauthorized assignment of the Franchise Agreement, the franchise, or ownership of the franchise;

9.2.8 Failure to Comply with Agreement. Repeatedly fails to comply with the Franchise Agreement, whether or not such failures are corrected, after notice thereof is delivered to the Franchise;

9.2.9 Misrepresentations. Has made any material misrepresentations or misstatements on Franchisee's application for the franchise or with respect to the ownership of the Franchisee;

9.2.10 Criminal Misconduct. Has engaged in criminal misconduct relevant to the reputation or operation of the business;

9.2.11 Failure to Adhere to Agreement. Fails to adhere to any material provision of the Franchise Agreement including, but not limited to, all payments Franchisee is required to pay to Franchisor as specified in Sections 3 and 7 of this Agreement, or any specification, standard, or operating procedure prescribed by Franchisor and does not correct such failure within fifteen (15) days after notice of same by Franchisor;

9.2.12 Noncompliance with Law. Fails to correct any noncompliance with any law or government regulation within five days of notice by the appropriate government agency or by Franchisor;

9.2.13 Failure to Meet Minimum Standards. In the event performance of Franchisee falls below the minimum operation standards set forth in this Agreement or in any Policy and Procedures Manual, Franchisee will be notified in writing setting forth such deficiency and, at the option of Franchisor, Franchisee may be placed on probation for a period of not less than 30 days and not more than 90 days. If such deficiency is not corrected within said probationary period, Franchisor may, at its option, terminate this Agreement.

9.3 Termination by Franchisor and Franchisee. This Agreement may be terminated by mutual written consent of the parties upon such terms and conditions as they may mutually agree.

9.4 Post-termination Obligations of Franchisee. On the termination or refusal to renew or extend the Franchise Agreement by Franchisor, the Franchisee shall cease to be an authorized Franchisee and shall:

9.4.1 Payment of Fees and Charges. Pay fees and charges due within seven days;

9.4.2 Discontinue Use of Marks. Immediately and permanently discontinue the use of all names and marks indicating or tending to indicate that the Franchisee is an authorized Franchisee. All signs, stationery, letterheads, forms, manuals, printed matter, and advertising containing Franchisor's marks shall promptly be surrendered to Franchisor. Franchisor shall pay Franchisee's costs for all such items surrendered;

9.4.3 Cease Advertising. Cease all advertising as an authorized Franchisee, including, but not limited to, the immediate removal of all signs from its premises;

9.4.4 Return of Franchisor's Property. Immediately return all Franchisor's Policy and Procedures Manuals, books, films, cassettes, forms, or brochures to Franchisor;

9.4.5 Books and Records. Maintain all books, records, and reports required by Franchisor for a period of not less than one year after termination;

9.4.6 Permit Inspection. Allow Franchisor to make final inspection of said books and records during normal business hours within a one-year period for the purpose of verifying that all fees or other expenses due Franchisor have been paid;

9.4.7 Cease Representations Regarding Relationship. Refrain from doing anything that would indicate that it is or ever was an authorized Franchisee;

9.4.8 Covenant Not to Compete. Abide by all provisions of the covenant not to compete under Section 18;

9.4.9 Assignment of Property. At the option of Franchisor assign the leased premises and telephone numbers of the franchise business to Franchisor or any party designated by it.

9.5 Franchisee's Business Property. Upon termination or refusal to renew or extend the Franchise Agreement by Franchisor or by the Franchisee, the Franchisee retains (unless the leased premises are, upon Franchisor's option, assigned to Franchisor or a party designated by it) its business property, location, site, furnishings, inventory, etc. except that all indications of Franchisor's affiliation must be removed.

SECTION 10. DEATH OF FRANCHISEE

10.1 Successor. In the event of the death of the Franchisee (who owns or controls 50% or more of the franchise business) during the term of this Agreement, Franchisor agrees that such person as shall be determined by Franchisee's will, or, in the event of Franchisee's intestacy, under the law of succession in effect in the state in which the deceased Franchisee's property interest in the franchise is located, to be the successor to the interest in the deceased Franchisee's property interest in the franchise (hereinafter referred to as "Successor"), shall be granted a franchise for the balance of the term of this Agreement subject to the following:

10.1.1 Application and Qualification. Successor may apply to Franchisor for acceptance by Franchisor and, if determined to be qualified in accordance with then prevailing standards, and upon compliance with the conditions described in subparagraph (c) below, such Successor shall be granted the franchise for the balance of the term, for the previously agreed territory.

10.1.2 Alternative for Qualification. If Successor is not willing or able to qualify as a Franchisee, such Successor may apply to Franchisor for acceptance by Franchisor by designating an individual employed by such Successor to be qualified in accordance with the then prevailing standards, and upon compliance with the conditions described in Section 10.2 below, such Successor shall be granted the franchise for the balance of the term, for the previously agreed territory.

10.2 Acceptance of Successor. The acceptance of the Successor as a Franchisee is subject to the following conditions:

10.2.1 Delinquent Obligations. Payment of delinquent obligations of the deceased Franchisee or his or her estate, if any, pertaining to this Agreement;

10.2.2 Assumption by Successor. Written assumption by the Successor, in forms furnished or approved by Franchisor of the obligations of the Franchisee under this Agreement;

10.2.3 Execution of Other Documents. Execution by Successor of such other documents as may be reasonably required by Franchisor;

10.2.4 Training Requirements. Compliance with the training requirements for franchisees set forth in this Agreement, and the payment of a training fee of not more than $1,000 prior to the training session.

10.3 Transfer to Others. Any proposed transfer of this franchise by the legal representative of the estate of the deceased

Franchisee to a person other than a Successor who qualified as a Franchisee, in accordance with Sections 10.1 and 10.2, shall be subject to the provisions governing assignment as set forth elsewhere in this Agreement.

10.4 Failure to Transfer. If no Successor shall have qualified and no transfer of the franchise shall have otherwise been accomplished consistent with the foregoing provisions within six months from the date of death of the Franchisee, Franchisor shall have the right to terminate this Agreement but may exercise any option it possesses under this Agreement or under the terms of the Franchisee's lease in order to maintain the operation of the business as a company-owned operation.

10.5 Court Order. Franchisor shall have the right to require a certified copy of an order of the court having jurisdiction over the deceased Franchisee's estate in which the Successor shall be determined, and may rely on such certified copy for the purposes of this paragraph. If not furnished with such certified copy of a court order, or in the event of a legal contest, Franchisor may decline, without liability, to recognize the claim of a party to be Successor. Franchisor shall not be liable to any heir, next of kin, devisee, legatee, or legal representative of a deceased Franchisee by reason of acceptance of a surviving spouse or child of the deceased Franchisee as Successor, provided such acceptance is not contrary to the order of a court of competent jurisdiction served on Franchisor.

10.6 Interim Operation. During the interim period from the date of death of Franchisee until qualification of Successor, or until a transfer of the franchise shall have otherwise been accomplished consistent with this Section 10, the legal representative shall operate under this Franchise Agreement through an individual who has the requisite qualifications for interim management thereof, as determined by Franchisor, it being understood that should the legal representative have failed to designate an individual so qualifying within 90 days after the death of the Franchisee, Franchisor shall have the right to terminate this Agreement but may exercise any option it may possess under this Agreement or under the terms of the Franchisee's lease in order to maintain the operation of the business as a company-owned operation.

10.7 State Law. In the event any provisions of this Agreement pertaining to renewal, termination, or modification conflict with any controlling state law, such provision shall be subordinate to such state law, to the extent there is a conflict.

SECTION 11. ASSIGNMENT OF THE FRANCHISE

11.1 Agreement Is Personal. This Agreement is personal, being entered into in reliance upon and in consideration of the skill, qualifications, and representations of, and the trust and confidence reposed in, Franchisee and Franchisee's present partners or officers (if Franchisee is a partnership or corporation), who will actively and substantially participate in the operation of the franchise business.

11.2 Limitations on Transfer. Neither this Agreement, the franchise, nor any part of the ownership of the franchise (which shall mean and include voting stock, securities convertible thereto, proprietorship interest, and general partnership interest) may be voluntarily, directly, or indirectly assigned or otherwise transferred or encumbered by the Franchisee or its owners (including without limitation by will, declaration of or transfer in trust, or by the laws of intestate succession) except as provided herein without the prior written approval of Franchisor, and any such assignment, transfer, or encumbrance without such approval constitutes a breach of this Agreement. Franchisor will not, however, unreasonably withhold consent to an assignment if the conditions specified below are met:

11.2.1 Satisfaction With Assignee. Franchisor is satisfied with the character, business experience, and credit rating of the proposed assignee (and its partners, officers, and/or controlling stockholders);

11.2.2 Payment of Debts. Payment of all outstanding debts to Franchisor (or its designated suppliers) by the assigning Franchisee;

11.2.3 Release. A general release of claims by the franchise and Franchisee;

11.2.4 Execution of Agreement. Assignee's execution of the then current Franchise Agreement;

11.2.5 Transfer Fee. Payment by assignee of a $1,000 transfer fee;

11.2.6 Training Program. Attendance by the proposed assignee or a managing employee at the next available New Franchise Training Program at assignee's expense and the payment of a $1,000 training fee prior to the training session;

11.2.7 Compliance With Law. Completion of the steps necessary, if any, to comply with the Federal Trade Commission Rules and/or state laws regarding franchising.

11.3 Incorporation of Franchisee's Business. If the Franchisee is a sole proprietorship or partnership, and if the conditions of Sections 11.2.1-11.2.4 and 11.2.7 (except 11.2.5 and 11.2.6) are met, Franchisor will consent to the assignment without payment of a transfer fee of this Agreement to a corporation formed, owned, and controlled solely by the Franchisee to operate the franchise business, provided such assignment shall not relieve the original Franchisee of the obligations of this Agreement.

11.4 Transfer of Interests in Franchisee's Business.

11.4.1 Corporation. If the Franchisee is a corporation, any merger thereof, or sale or transfer of more than 49% of any one class of stock or any series (whether related or unrelated) or sales or transfers totalling in the aggregate 49% or more of any one class of stock in such corporate Franchisee, whether by operation of law or otherwise, shall be deemed an attempted assignment of this Agreement requiring the prior written consent of Franchisor.

11.4.2 Partnership. If the Franchisee is a partnership, the sale or transfer of any general partner's interest or the sale or series of sales or transfers of limited partnership interests totalling in such aggregate 49% of such interests (including transfers of shares in corporate partners) whether by operation of law or otherwise, shall be deemed an attempted assignment of this agreement and shall require the prior written consent of Franchisor.

11.4.3 Aggregation of Transfers. For the purpose of determining whether 49% or more of the interests of any class of shares or of general partnership interests have been transferred, all transfers (whether related or unrelated) shall be aggregated. Any proposed transfer involving less than 49% but more than 25% of the stock or general partnership interests of the Franchisee shall be reported by the Franchisee to Franchisor at lease 20 days in advance of any such transfer but shall not be subject to the approval of Franchisor.

11.5 Assignment by Franchisor. Franchisor reserves the right to assign the Franchise Agreement provided that such assignment shall not affect the rights and privileges of the Franchisee under the agreement.

11.6 Right of First Refusal. Franchisor has the right of first refusal on any proposed assignment by Franchisee. Franchisee shall serve upon Franchisor a written notice setting forth all of the terms and conditions of the proposed assignment, a suitable current financial statement regarding the proposed assignee, and all other information requested by Franchisor concerning the proposed assignee. Said notice shall provide Franchisor with sufficient time to enable Franchisor to comply with all disclosure requirements with respect to any intended assignee. Within 20 days after receipt of such notice (or if Franchisor requests additional information, within 15 days after receipt of such additional information), Franchisor may either consent or refuse to consent to the assignment or, at its option, accept the assignment to itself upon the same terms and conditions specified in said notice. Consent to an assignment upon the specified terms and conditions shall not be deemed to be a consent to an assignment upon any other terms or conditions, nor to any other person, nor to any other subsequent assignment.

SECTION 12. REMEDIES FOR BREACH, ATTORNEY FEES, AND FORCE MAJEURE

12.1 Remedies. Franchisee expressly consents and agrees that Franchisor may, in addition to any other available remedies, obtain an injunction without bond to terminate or prevent the continuation of any existing default or violation, and to prevent the occurrence of any threatened default or violation of this Agreement.

12.2 Attorney's Fees. If any legal action shall be instituted to interpret or enforce the terms and conditions of this Agreement, the prevailing party shall be entitled to recover its costs and reasonable attorney's fees.

12.3 Force Majeure. Neither Franchisor or Franchisee shall be liable to each other, or be deemed in breach or default of any obligation contained in this Agreement, for any delay or failure to perform for difficulties of performance occasioned by war, law, regulations or order of public authority, labor troubles, shortages of materials, acts of God, or other causes amounting to Force Majeure.

SECTION 13. MODIFICATIONS

13.1 Terms and Conditions. This Agreement contains all of the terms and conditions agreed upon by the parties hereto. No promises or representations have been made other than as herein set forth.

13.2 Modifications. Any modification or change in this Agreement must be in writing executed by Franchisee and an officer of Franchisor authorized by the Board of Directors of Franchisor. No field representative or any other employee of Franchisor has the right or authority to make oral or written modifications of this Agreement, and any such modifications shall not be binding upon either party hereto.

SECTION 14. WAIVER

No waiver of any breach of any condition, covenant, or agreement contained in this Agreement shall constitute a waiver of any subsequent breach of the same or any other condition, covenant, or agreement.

SECTION 15. MISCELLANEOUS

15.1 Governing Law. This Agreement shall be governed by the laws of the State of _____, and Franchisee expressly and freely agrees that should any legal action against Franchisor be necessary, all such action shall be taken exclusively in the State of _____. Franchisee hereby submits himself/herself/itself to the jurisdiction of the courts of _____ County, _____.

15.2 Partial Invalidity. In case any one or more of the provisions of this Agreement or any application thereof shall be invalid, illegal, or unenforceable in any respect, the validity, legality, and enforceability of the remaining provisions contained in this Agreement and any other application thereof shall not in any way be affected or impaired thereby.

15.3 Headings. Section and subsection headings are for reference purposes only and shall not in any way modify or limit the statements contained in any section or subsection.

15.4 Number and Gender. All words in this Agreement shall be deemed to include any number or gender as the context or sense of this Agreement requires. All references herein to Franchisee or Franchisor shall include the plural if there be more than one, and the masculine, feminine, or neuter as the case may be.

15.5 Conflict With Manual. In the event of any conflict between this Agreement and the Policy and Procedures Manual, this Agreement shall control.

SECTION 16. AUTHORITY AND ACCEPTANCE

16.1 Warranty of Authority. Each of the undersigned parties warrants that he/she/it has full authority to sign and execute this Agreement.

16.2 Acceptance. This Agreement shall become valid on the date it is accepted by Franchisor. Franchisor will notify Franchisee of such acceptance by sending Franchisee an executed copy of the Agreement. If this Agreement is not accepted by Franchisor within 60 days of receipt, then all monies paid hereunder shall be returned to the Franchisee and this Agreement shall be null and void, unless the parties agree in writing to a longer period.

SECTION 17. DISCLAIMER OF WARRANTIES AND ENTIRE AGREEMENT

17.1 Representations. Franchisee represents, warrants, and acknowledges that Franchisor, its officers, employees, and/or agents, have made no representations or warranties, expressed or implied, as to the profitability of a franchise business. Franchisee further acknowledges that Franchisee has conducted Franchisee's own independent investigation as to the desirability of entering into this transaction and that Franchisee has had full opportunity to seek independent legal counsel and financial advice with respect to entering into this Agreement. Franchisee specifically states that Franchisee has not relied upon oral or verbal representations of Franchisor, its officers, employees, and/or agents in deciding to purchase this franchise.

17.2 Uniform Offering Circular. FRANCHISEE ACKNOWLEDGES THAT HE/SHE/IT HAS RECEIVED, AT THE EARLIER OF THE FIRST PERSONAL MEETING WITH FRANCHISOR OR TEN (10) BUSINESS DAYS PRIOR TO THE EXECUTION BY FRANCHISEE OF THIS AGREEMENT OR PAYMENT OF ANY CONSIDER-

ATION TO FRANCHISOR, A COPY OF THE CURRENT FRANCHISOR'S UNIFORM FRANCHISE OFFERING CIRCULAR FOR THE STATE IN WHICH FRANCHISEE'S AREA IS LOCATED.

17.3 Understanding of Agreement. FRANCHISEE STATES THAT HE/SHE/IT HAS RECEIVED, READ AND UNDERSTOOD THIS AGREEMENT, AND HAS BEEN ACCORDED AN AMPLE OPPORTUNITY AND A PERIOD OF NOT LESS THAN FIVE (5) BUSINESS DAYS AFTER RECEIPT OF A FINAL COPY OF THIS AGREEMENT TO CONSULT WITH ADVISORS OF HIS OR HER OWN CHOOSING CONCERNING THE POTENTIAL BENEFITS AND RISKS THAT MAY BE INVOLVED IN ENTERING INTO THIS AGREEMENT AND BECOMING A FRANCHISEE.

17.4 Financial Statements. FRANCHISEE HAS PROVIDED FRANCHISOR WITH ACCURATE FINANCIAL STATEMENTS, WHICH PRESENT A TRUE REPRESENTATION OF FRANCHISEE'S FINANCIAL CONDITION.

17.5 Stock Certificate Legend. Franchisee, if it is a corporation, acknowledges that no stock of the corporation may be transferred without Franchisor's prior approval in accordance with Section 11. Franchisee agrees to place the following legend on all certificates of stock in the corporation: The transfer of this stock is subject to the terms and conditions of a Franchise Agreement with _____, a[n] _____ [state of incorporation] corporation, as Franchisor.

17.6 Entire Agreement. This Agreement represents and constitutes the entire agreement between the parties. All other representations or negotiations, past or present, verbal or written, are merged herein.

SECTION 18. AGREEMENT NOT TO COMPETE OR DISCLOSE

18.1 Covenant Not to Compete. As long as this Agreement shall be in effect, and for a period of two years thereafter, regardless of the cause of termination, the Franchisee shall not in any capacity, directly or indirectly, engage or be financially interested in or associated with any business similar or substantially similar to a _____ business within a 50 mile radius of the exclusive territory granted Franchisee, any exclusive territory granted to other Franchisees, or any company-owned location, or employ or seek to employ any person who at the time of his employment is employed, or at any time six months prior thereto has been employed, by any other franchise business or by Franchisor.

18.2 Nondisclosure. At no time, except in the normal course of the Franchisee's business hereunder, shall the Franchisee disclose to any person any information or knowledge concerning the methods of promotion, sale, or distribution used by Franchisor.

18.3 Remedies. In addition to any other remedies available, Franchisor shall be entitled to obtain an injunction without bond to terminate or prevent the continuation of any existing or continuing default or violation of Sections 18.1 or 18.2.

SECTION 19. NOTICES

19.1 Form. Any notices to be given hereunder shall be in writing, and may be delivered personally, or by certified or registered mail, with postage fully prepaid. Any notice delivered by mail in the manner herein specified shall be deemed delivered five days after mailing or, if earlier, on actual receipt.

19.2 Addresses. Any notices to be delivered to Franchisor shall be addressed to [address]. Any notice to Franchisee shall be delivered to the address set forth in the first paragraph of this Agreement.

19.3 Change of Notice Address. The address specified herein for service of notices may be changed at any time by the party making the change giving written notice to the other party.

SECTION 20. EXCLUSIVE PROPERTY

The form and content of this Agreement are the exclusive property of Franchisor and may not be reproduced in part or in whole by Franchisee.

SECTION 21. ADDITIONAL REPRESENTATIONS

21.1 Franchisee's Representations and Warranties. Franchisee makes the following additional warranties and representations:

21.1.1 Form of Business Organization. Franchisee is a _____ [corporation, partnership, or sole proprietorship].

21.1.2 Beneficial Ownership. If Franchisee is a corporation or partnership, there is set forth below the name and address of each shareholder or partner in the franchise holding 10% or more interest in the corporation or partnership.

21.2 Protected Territory Description. Franchisor agrees that no other franchise or company-owned operation will be sold or operated in the protected territory consisting of: (Map attached) The Minimum Number of Initial Targeted Households for

Franchisee's exclusive territory is:_____.

IN WITNESS WHEREOF, the parties hereto have caused this Agreement to be executed on the date first set forth above.

FRANCHISEE: _____

BY: _____

TITLE: _____ DATE: _____

SIGNATURE: _____

FRANCHISOR: _____

BY: _____

TITLE: _____ DATE: _____

SIGNATURE: _____

accountants, 52, 59, 64, 69, 70, 73, 74, 75, 76, 78, 80, 89, 100, 149, 170, 172

advertising funds, 11, 62, 94, 107, 161, 169, 170, 188, 194

advertising network, 11, 12

affiliates, 56, 87, 123, 151, 153

American Association of Franchisees and Dealers, 27, 28, 139, 140

American Bar Association's Forum Committee on Franchising, 30, 76

American Franchisee Association, 27, 139, 140

appendix, 4, 49, 55, 56, 61, 62, 64, 86, 91, 105, 107, 108, 110, 111, 112, 113, 114, 116, 117, 120, 122, 125, 127, 128

arbitration, 110, 128, 129, 130, 131, 135, 146

Arkansas, 41, 182

associations, 26, 27, 28, 30, 55, 56, 68, 76, 93, 124, 139, 140, 141, 143

attorneys, 39, 40, 52, 56, 74, 75, 76, 80, 110, 111, 136, 188, 209, 210

bankruptcy, 56, 58, 88, 118, 131, 151, 157, 182, 200

brokers, 69, 79, 80, 163

business experience, 13, 56, 121, 151, 154, 155, 207

business opportunity laws, 40

business plan, 75

California, 19, 20, 27, 29, 38, 39, 41, 42, 182

choice of law, 128, 130

computers, 8, 14, 15, 23, 26, 68, 89, 115, 172, 173, 174

computerization, 14, 15

Connecticut, 39, 41, 42, 182

Delaware, 41, 182

disclosure document, 4, 30, 38, 39, 40, 49, 50, 51, 52, 53, 54, 55, 56, 60, 62, 63, 65, 67, 73, 74, 75, 77, 80, 81, 86, 88, 89, 91, 97, 143, 149

earnings claims, 4, 57, 69, 80, 97, 98, 99, 100, 152, 183

encroachment, 127, 140

Federal Trade Commission, 20, 31, 147, 148, 149, 207

fees, 7, 11, 12, 18, 19, 20, 21, 23, 56, 59, 60, 68, 70, 75, 77, 80, 112, 113, 116, 117, 118, 119, 133, 146, 151, 157, 158, 159, 160, 161, 163, 167, 171, 172, 187, 188, 192, 193, 195, 197, 198, 199, 200, 202, 207, 209, 210

financing, 57, 75, 109, 113, 115, 151, 162, 166, 174

financial projections, 67
financial statements, 55, 57, 63, 64, 65, 75, 84, 86, 118, 152, 170, 171, 172, 183, 196, 200, 209, 213
Florida, 39, 42
Forum on Franchising, 30, 76
forum selection clauses, 130
franchise brokers, 79, 80
franchisee councils, 95, 138, 141
franchisee network, 13, 18
franchisee's obligations, 57, 151, 189
franchisor's obligations, 57, 151, 166
franchise agreement, 4, 28, 55, 56, 62, 63, 64, 65, 74, 75, 77, 81, 93, 105, 106, 107, 108, 109, 110, 111, 112, 114, 115, 116, 117, 118, 119, 120, 121, 122, 125, 126, 127, 128, 129, 130, 131, 133, 135, 137, 140, 144, 145, 146, 147, 148, 152, 154, 155, 158, 163, 166, 167, 168, 169, 170, 171, 172, 173, 174, 176, 177, 178, 179, 180, 181, 182, 184, 185, 198, 199, 200, 201, 202, 203, 205, 207, 208, 213
franchise associations, 26, 27, 139, 143
Franchise Offering Circular, 55, 56, 145, 213
FTC, 19, 20, 31, 32, 37, 38, 39, 49, 50, 51, 52, 53, 54, 55, 73, 89, 91, 97, 139, 143, 147, 148, 149, 207
FTC disclosure document , 73
FTC Rule, 20, 38, 39, 49, 50, 51, 91, 97

Georgia, 39

Hawaii, 21, 39, 41, 42, 43, 182
history of franchisor, 83–90

IFA, 26, 27, 139, 140
Illinois, 20, 28, 39, 41, 43, 53, 182

Indiana, 20, 39, 41, 43, 130, 131, 182
informational imbalance, 3, 37, 143
initial franchise fee, 21, 56, 112, 113, 146, 151, 157, 158, 163, 187, 193
initial investment, 57, 60, 146, 151, 161, 162
International Franchise Association, 26, 27
investigation of franchisees, 91–95
investigation of franchisor, 41, 54, 55, 80, 86, 138, 144, 212
Iowa, 39, 41, 43, 139, 140, 182

Kentucky, 44

lawsuits, 127
lawyers, 73, 74, 75, 76, 77, 78, 130, 131, 149
litigation, 56, 58, 64, 65, 87, 88, 89, 129, 135, 146, 151, 157, 178, 179

Maine, 39
Maryland, 20, 39, 44
Michigan, 20, 39, 41, 44, 53, 182
Minnesota, 20, 21, 39, 41, 44, 182
Mississippi, 41, 182
Missouri, 41, 182

NASAA, 56, 143
Nebraska, 45, 182
negotiation of franchise agreement, 63, 106, 109, 110, 111
New Hampshire, 39
New Jersey, 41, 156, 157, 182
New York, 20, 38, 45
North American Securities Administrators Association, 56
North Carolina, 39
North Dakota, 20, 39, 45

Offering Circular, 49, 50, 51, 53, 54, 55, 56, 61, 77, 84, 86, 98, 99,

106, 110, 111, 112, 113, 125, 126, 145, 146, 147, 148, 153, 157, 165, 177, 178, 181, 182, 183, 184, 186, 212, 213
Ohio, 45
Oklahoma, 39
operations manuals, 94, 108, 125
outlets, 11, 57, 116, 124, 134, 152, 177, 183

patents, 57, 63, 151, 178, 180
"plain english" requirement, 56, 106
product and equipment purchase requirements, 122
professional assistance, 24, 40, 50, 63, 65, 70, 73, 74, 75, 88
proprietary information, 57, 151, 180
proven format, 2, 9, 10, 12, 13
public figures, 57, 152, 182
purchase price negotiations, 112, 113

questions for existing franchisees, 59, 69

receipt for offering circular, 57, 152, 184
registration of franchises, 38, 52
restrictions on sources of products and services, 57, 123, 151, 163
Rhode Island, 20, 39, 46
risk factors, 146
renewal, 57, 63, 94, 109, 112, 113, 114, 115, 116, 117, 152, 164, 181, 182, 198, 199, 206
relationship laws, 41, 120

specialization, 9, 10
South Carolina, 39

South Dakota, 21, 39, 41, 46, 182
state administrators, 52, 147, 152

termination, 41, 57, 63, 115, 117, 118, 119, 120, 125, 135, 136, 140, 152, 181, 182, 187, 189, 198, 199, 200, 201, 202, 203, 206, 214
termination laws, 135, 206
territory, 57, 73, 108, 109, 112, 113, 116, 126, 127, 146, 151, 154, 157, 158, 166, 176, 190, 192, 204, 214, 215, 216
territory, encroachment, 127, 140
Texas, 39, 46
trademarks, 19, 20, 21, 57, 60, 63, 107, 134, 145, 151, 172, 176, 177, 178, 179, 180, 181, 185, 188, 189, 190, 191, 196
training, 7, 12, 13, 18, 23, 60, 61, 62, 72, 94, 108, 121, 125, 134, 152, 158, 160, 162, 163, 167, 168, 174, 175, 176, 180, 181, 192, 196, 197, 198, 204, 207

UFOC, 55, 56, 58, 59, 61, 62, 64, 65, 69, 86, 87, 91, 98, 111, 113, 122, 124, 125
UFOC guidelines, 56, 64, 98, 113, 125
Uniform Franchise Offering Circular, 55, 56, 213
uniform system, 10, 11
Utah, 39, 46, 47

Virginia, 20, 39, 41, 47, 182

Washington, 21, 27, 30, 39, 41, 43, 47, 148, 149, 182
web sites, 15, 27, 70
Wisconsin, 20, 39, 41, 47, 53, 182

OTHER FRANCHISE TITLES
FROM PILOT BOOKS!

Directory of Franchising Organizations. New Expanded 1998 Edition. Lists over 2,200 successful franchises, including concise descriptions, investment required, important facts about franchising and evaluation checklist. 208 pages. ISBN: 0-87576-215-8. $12.95

OTHER BUSINESS TITLES
FROM PILOT BOOKS!

the bare-bones guide to Better Business Writing by Sally Williams. The book you'll constantly refer to when writing business letters, memos, presentations or proposals for questions on grammar, punctuation and vocabulary. 40 pages. ISBN: 0-87576-203-4. $7.95

The Directory of Home-Based Business Resources by Priscilla Y. Huff. A tightly organized, extensive reference book on where to find information on everything needed to succeed in a home-based business. 36 pages. ISBN: 0-87576-200-X. $7.95

The Where-To-Sell-It Directory–1997/1998 Edition. Where to find dealers and collectors who will buy almost anything by mail, from appliances to weapons. Includes important tips on how to sell by mail. 64 pages. ISBN: 0-87576-198-4. $7.95

To order, call: (800) 79-PILOT, fax: 516-477-0978, e-mail: feed back@pilotbooks.com or write us at Pilot Books, 127 Sterling Ave., P.O. Box 2102, Greenport, NY 11944. Please add $3.50 postage and handling for each title shipped. We accept personal checks and Master Card or Visa payments.